THE AUSTRALIAN
Women's Weekly
pies
savoury & sweet

Contents

The oven temperatures in this book are for conventional ovens; if you have a fan-forced oven, decrease the temperature by 10-20 degrees.

pastry

Pastry is one of those things in the culinary world that is well worth mastering – especially the ever-popular shortcrust pastry, be it sweet or savoury. Frozen sheets of various types of pastry, including sweet and savoury shortcrust, are readily available in supermarkets and no home freezer should be without them for those last-minute tops for pies, turnovers and pasties. Goodies made using pastry are usually eaten in the cooler months; ideally, pastry should always be made in a cool kitchen. Allow yourself time to make pastry; it's well worth it.

Like everything else, particularly in the baking area, there are some rules involved. Use a good basic recipe like the one opposite and follow the recipe and the rules very carefully.

Perfect pastry has a "look" and a "feel" to it – it should be easy to handle and easy to roll without major cracks. Try to remember the way it looked and felt, then aim to come up with that same result every time; it's a good idea to make notes to yourself on the recipe.

Cool fingertips with a light touch make good pastry, hot hands and heavy handling don't. Food processors make good pastry too, providing the ingredients are "pulsed" together using short bursts of power; process only until the ingredients cling together.

Over-handling or over-processing will result in tough, hard-to-roll pastry; it will develop large cracks during the rolling process.

basic shortcrust pastry

1½ cups (225g) plain (all-purpose) flour
125g (4 ounces) cold butter, chopped coarsely
1 egg yolk
2 tablespoons iced water, approximately

HAND-MADE METHOD
Sift flour into large bowl, rub in butter with fingertips. Add egg yolk and enough of the water to make ingredients barely cling together. Knead pastry lightly on floured surface until smooth; press into a disc shape. Enclose pastry in plastic wrap, refrigerate 30 minutes.

PROCESSOR METHOD
Sift flour into processor bowl, add butter, pulse, until mixture is crumbly. Add egg yolk and most of the water, pulse until ingredients barely cling together, add more water if necessary. Knead pastry lightly on floured surface until smooth; press into disc shape. Enclose pastry in plastic wrap, refrigerate 30 minutes.

Sweet shortcrust pastry variation: Sift 2 tablespoons icing (confectioners') sugar with the flour.
Note: This recipe makes the equivalent of two sheets of store-bought shortcrust pastry.

About the ingredients:

All the ingredients and even the mixing bowl, should be chilled.

Flour

Weigh or measure the flour, add a pinch of salt if you like, sift it into a mixing bowl – or the bowl of a food processor – then refrigerate it for about 30 minutes.
Icing sugar: Add it to the sifter with the flour (and salt) for sweet shortcrust pastry.

Butter

The butter must be very cold, even partly frozen. Chop it into 1cm cubes, or, if it's hard and cold enough, coarsely grate it, then place it into either the mixing or food processor bowl.
Rub the butter through the flour using fingertips, or pulse the processor until the butter is evenly distributed through the flour. The mixture should be slightly coarse, not too fine, or the butter and flour will come together before any liquid is added.

Egg yolk, lemon juice, water

Usually one or two of these ingredients is used to bind the flour and butter mixture together. The secret to making perfect pastry is knowing just how much of these ingredients to add; this knowledge comes with experience.
Insufficient liquid will result in a pastry that is crumbly and almost impossible to roll out; it will develop large cracks during the rolling process. Too much liquid will make the pastry too soft and sticky and the pastry will shrink during baking. Most recipes will suggest an approximate amount of liquid; it's a judgment call and, each time pastry is made the amount of liquid needed will vary slightly. This is due to the rate at which the flour absorbs the liquid: old flour (more dehydrated) will absorb more liquid than new (less dehydrated) flour.
The liquid should be added as fast as possible – that is, preferably in one batch, not in small amounts. Once again, over-handling or over-processing will result in tough pastry. Practice makes (for) perfect (pastry).

step-by-step

Cool ingredients, cool fingertips and a light touch are the keys to perfect pastry.

Kneading pastry

Strictly speaking, pastry isn't really kneaded as a bread dough would be kneaded, it's just quickly and lightly shaped into a block or disc for the resting process.

Use the least amount of flour possible when shaping the pastry, just enough to stop the dough sticking to the bench or board.

Marble is the perfect surface on which to handle pastry and stainless steel is quite good too, but a laminated, tiled or timber surface works well enough.

Resting pastry

The resting time in the refrigerator for pastry is usually about 30 minutes – this is vital for success. During this time, the protein (gluten) in the flour relaxes, resulting in pastry that feels great in the mouth.

Resting is usually done straight after the pastry is made. Shape the pastry into a block or disc, the same thickness all the way through, enclose the pastry in plastic wrap and refrigerate for the time stated in the recipe. A lot of recipes suggest another resting after the pastry has been rolled out and the dish lined (the ideal time is usually 20 to 30 minutes). Some recipes suggest freezing the pastry for the last resting. Once again this resting allows the now-slightly-stretched pastry – due to the rolling-out process – time to relax; it also helps to minimise shrinkage during the baking process.

Rolling pastry

This is done either on the bench, using a minimum amount of flour to prevent sticking – excess flour simply upsets the balance of the ingredients – or between sheets of baking or greaseproof paper.

There are many types, sizes and shapes of rolling pins available, made from wood, ceramic, plastic or glass; all work well. It's important when pastry is being rolled out that an even pressure is used to try and keep the pastry the same thickness all the way through. Roll in short light strokes from the centre out to the edge of the pastry; never roll over the edge of the pastry or it may become too thin and difficult to lift off the paper.

Lining a dish or tin

If the pastry has been rolled out on the bench, place the rolling pin in the centre of the pastry, flap half the pastry over the pin, hold the pin up with one hand, supporting the pastry underneath with the other hand.
Lift the pastry over the dish and ease it over the base, remove the pin, then gently push the pastry around the side of the dish, without stretching it.
If the pastry has been rolled between sheets of baking paper, remove the top layer of paper, support the pastry underneath the remaining paper, then turn the pastry into the dish. Peel the paper away and ease the pastry around the side of the dish.
Trim the edge of the pastry by rolling the pin over the dish.

Docking pastry

Some recipes require the pastry to be "docked" to prevent it rising. Prick the pastry all over, about 2cm apart, using a fork or a pastry docker. If the pastry case is in a dish with a deep side like a pie dish, prick the side or wall of the pastry as well as the base.

Baking blind

Sometimes it is necessary to bake the pastry blind (ie cook it without a filling). For best results, follow individual recipes. Line the uncooked pastry case with either a piece of foil or baking paper, fill the cavity with uncooked rice, pulses or ceramic or metal beads. This is to weight the pastry evenly to prevent rising during the baking. Bake the pastry case for the specified time. Remove the dish from the oven, carefully lift the foil or paper up to remove the weights from the pastry case to the bench. Leave the weights to cool completely before sealing in an airtight container for future use; don't use for cooking. Return the pastry case to the oven for further baking. Usually the whole baking blind process takes between 15 and 20 minutes.

poultry pies

chinese duck & five-spice pies

2kg (4-pound) whole duck
1 tablespoon vegetable oil
4 shallots (100g), chopped finely
2 tablespoons plain (all-purpose) flour
½ cup (125ml) chicken stock
¼ cup (60ml) chinese cooking wine
2 tablespoons light soy sauce
2 tablespoons orange juice
2 teaspoons light brown sugar
4 cinnamon sticks
1 egg, beaten lightly

FIVE-SPICE PASTRY
2 cups (300g) plain (all-purpose) flour
2 teaspoons finely grated orange rind
½ teaspoon five-spice powder
125g (4 ounces) butter, chopped coarsely
1 egg
1 tablespoon water

1   Rinse duck under cold water. Place duck in large saucepan; cover with cold water. Bring to the boil, uncovered, reduce heat; simmer, covered, 30 minutes. Cool in water in pan. Remove meat from duck; discard skin and bones. Shred meat.
2   Meanwhile, make five-spice pastry.
3   Heat oil in large frying pan; cook shallot, stirring, until soft. Add flour; cook, stirring, 1 minute. Gradually stir in combined stock, wine, sauce, juice and sugar; bring to the boil. Simmer, uncovered, 3 minutes. Add duck; season to taste. Cool.
4   Preheat oven to 200°C/400°F. Grease four round pie tins (1-cup/250ml). Roll pastry between sheets of baking paper until large enough to line tins with 5cm (2 inches) of pastry overhanging. Lift pastry into tins, press into base and side. Divide duck mixture among pies. Fold excess pastry over filling to enclose. Position a cinnamon stick on each pie; brush with egg.
5   Bake about 25 minutes. Stand pies in tins for 5 minutes before serving.

FIVE-SPICE PASTRY Process flour, rind and five-spice until combined. Add butter; process until crumbly. Add egg and water; process until ingredients just come together. Knead dough on floured surface until smooth. Enclose in plastic wrap; refrigerate 30 minutes.

prep + cook time 1 hour 30 minutes
(+ cooling & refrigeration) makes 4
nutritional count per serving 139.2g total fat
(50.7g saturated fat); 7231kJ (1730 cal);
66.5g carbohydrate; 51g protein; 3.4g fibre

chicken, silver beet and egg pides

1 tablespoon olive oil
1 medium brown onion (150g), chopped finely
2 cloves garlic, crushed
4 stalks silver beet (swiss chard) (320g), shredded
1½ cups (240g) shredded cooked chicken
2 teaspoons ground coriander
2 tablespoons pistachios, roasted, chopped
½ cup coarsely chopped fresh coriander (cilantro)
4 eggs, beaten lightly
1 teaspoon each nigella and sesame seeds

DOUGH
2 cups (300g) plain (all-purpose) flour
1½ teaspoons (7g) dry yeast
½ teaspoon salt
¾ cup (180ml) water
1 tablespoon olive oil

1 Make dough.
2 Meanwhile, heat oil in large frying pan; cook onion and garlic, stirring, until onion softens. Add silver beet, chicken and ground coriander; cook, stirring, until silver beet wilts. Stir in nuts and chopped coriander. Season to taste.
3 Preheat oven to 220°C/425°F. Oil oven tray.
4 Turn dough onto floured surface; knead until smooth. Divide dough into four; roll into 18cm (7-inch) rounds. Spoon a quarter of the chicken mixture in centre of each round; brush edges with a little egg. Fold over edges to almost enclose filling, twisting ends to seal. Place on tray. Reserve 1 tablespoon egg; carefully pour remaining egg over chicken filling. Brush dough with reserved egg; sprinkle with seeds. Bake about 35 minutes or until browned.

DOUGH Combine flour, yeast and salt in large bowl; stir in the water and oil, mix to a soft dough. Knead dough on floured surface about 5 minutes or until smooth and elastic. Place dough in large oiled bowl, turn to coat in oil. Cover; stand in warm place about 1 hour or until dough doubles.

prep + cook time 1 hour 20 minutes (+ standing)
makes 4
nutritional count per serving 26.1g total fat (5.1g saturated fat); 2270kJ (543 cal); 40.9g carbohydrate; 33.3g protein; 5.9g fibre

country chicken and vegetable pie

2 tablespoons olive oil
500g (1 pound) chicken breast fillets,
  chopped coarsely
1 medium brown onion (150g), chopped coarsely
1 large carrot (180g), chopped coarsely
1 celery stalk (150g), trimmed, chopped coarsely
150g (5½ ounces) button mushrooms,
  sliced thickly
2 medium potatoes (400g), chopped coarsely
1 tablespoon plain (all-purpose) flour
½ cup (125ml) dry white wine
1 cup (250ml) chicken stock
⅓ cup (80ml) pouring cream
½ cup (60g) frozen peas
2 tablespoons coarsely chopped fresh
  flat-leaf parsley
1 sheet puff pastry
1 egg, beaten lightly

1 Preheat oven to 220°C/425°F. Oil 1.5-litre (6-cup)
ovenproof dish.
2 Heat half the oil in large saucepan; cook chicken
until browned lightly all over. Remove from pan.
3 Heat remaining oil in same pan; cook onion,
carrot, celery and mushrooms, stirring, until
vegetables soften. Add potato, cook for 1 minute.
Add flour; cook, stirring, until mixture bubbles
and thickens. Gradually stir in wine, boil, stirring,
1 minute. Return chicken to pan with stock; bring
to the boil. Simmer, uncovered, about 8 minutes
until potato is tender. Stir in cream, peas and
parsley; season to taste. Cool.
4 Spoon mixture into dish. Top with pastry. Trim
edge; brush with egg. Bake pie about 20 minutes.

prep + cook time 50 minutes (+ cooling) **serves** 4
nutritional count per serving 29.9g total fat
(8g saturated fat); 2441kJ (584 cal);
33.2g carbohydrate; 38.2g protein; 4.7g fibre

gooey chicken, brie and cranberry pies

2 teaspoons olive oil
200g (6½ ounces) chicken tenderloins
2 sheets shortcrust pastry
⅓ cup (100g) cranberry sauce
20g (¾ ounce) baby spinach leaves
100g (3 ounces) brie cheese, sliced thinly
1 egg, beaten lightly

1 Preheat oven to 220°C/425°F. Line oven tray with baking paper.
2 Heat oil in medium frying pan; season chicken. Cook chicken until browned and cooked through. Remove from pan; slice thinly. Cool.

3 Cut four 10cm (4-inch) rounds from one sheet of pastry. Place rounds on tray. Spread with sauce, leaving 1cm (½-inch) border. Top with spinach, chicken and cheese. Cut four 11cm (4½-inch) rounds from remaining pastry sheet. Cover filling; press pastry edges with a fork to seal.
4 Brush pastries with egg. Cut a small slit in centre of each pie. Bake about 20 minutes or until browned lightly.

prep + cook time 35 minutes (+ cooling) **makes** 4
nutritional count per serving 34.6g total fat (17.7g saturated fat); 2466kJ (590 cal); 46.9g carbohydrate; 23.1g protein; 1.7g fibre

serving suggestion Serve with salad.

butter chicken puffs

20g (¾ ounce) butter
1 small brown onion (80g), chopped finely
250g (8 ounces) minced (ground) chicken
1 small carrot (70g), grated coarsely
2 tablespoons butter chicken curry paste
2 tablespoons frozen peas
3 sheets puff pastry
1 egg, beaten lightly

1 Preheat oven to 220°C/425°F. Line oven tray with baking paper.
2 Melt butter in large frying pan; cook onion, stirring, until soft. Add chicken; cook, stirring, until browned. Add carrot, paste and peas; cook for 5 minutes.
3 Cut four 11cm (4½-inch) rounds from each pastry sheet. Place rounded tablespoons of mixture on one side of rounds. Fold over to form a semi-circle. Press edges together to seal; place on tray. Brush with egg; cut three slits in each puff.
4 Bake about 20 minutes or until browned.

prep + cook time 40 minutes **makes** 12
nutritional count per serving 14g total fat
(2.3g saturated fat); 928kJ (222 cal);
16.2g carbohydrate; 7.3g protein; 1.2g fibre

serving suggestion Serve with a yogurt and mint dipping sauce.

chicken, mushroom & tarragon pies

40g (1½ ounces) butter
200g (6½ ounces) button mushrooms, sliced
750g (1½ pounds) chicken thigh fillets,
  chopped coarsely
1 tablespoon plain (all-purpose) flour
¾ cup (180ml) chicken stock
1 tablespoon finely chopped fresh tarragon
1 egg, beaten lightly

TARRAGON PASTRY
1½ cups (225g) plain (all-purpose) flour
¼ cup (20g) finely grated parmesan cheese
2 tablespoons finely chopped fresh tarragon
125g (4 ounces) butter, chopped coarsely
1 egg
1 tablespoon iced water, approximately

1   Make tarragon pastry.
2   Melt butter in large frying pan; cook mushrooms,
stirring, until browned. Add chicken; cook, stirring,
until browned. Add flour; cook, stirring, 1 minute.
Gradually stir in stock; stir over heat until mixture
boils and thickens. Season; cool. Stir in tarragon.
3   Preheat oven to 200°C/400°F. Oil four
(1-cup/250ml) metal pie tins. Divide pastry in
half. Roll one half between sheets of baking
paper until large enough to line tins. Cut pastry
into four squares, lift into tins, press into base
and sides; trim edges.
4   Divide chicken mixture among pies. Roll
remaining pastry between sheets of baking paper.
Cut four 14cm (5½-inch) rounds from pastry; place
over chicken mixture. Press edges to seal. Refrigerate
20 minutes. Brush tops with egg; cut a slit in pies.
Bake about 30 minutes. Stand in pans 5 minutes.

TARRAGON PASTRY Process flour, cheese,
tarragon and butter until crumbly. Add egg and
enough of the water to make ingredients just come
together. Knead dough on floured surface until
smooth. Cover; refrigerate 30 minutes.

prep + cook time 1 hour 10 minutes
(+ refrigeration & cooling) makes 4
nutritional count per serving 52.6g total fat
(28.4g saturated fat); 3532kJ (845 cal);
43.9g carbohydrate; 48.9g protein; 3.5g fibre

chicken, fennel and celery pie

1 tablespoon olive oil
1 medium fennel bulb (300g), trimmed, sliced thinly
2 celery sticks (300g), trimmed, chopped coarsely
1 medium leek (350g), chopped coarsely
600g (1½ pounds) chicken breast fillets,
  chopped coarsely
1 clove garlic, crushed
2 tablespoons plain (all-purpose) flour
1 cup (250ml) chicken stock
½ cup (125ml) pouring cream
1 egg white

SOUR CREAM PASTRY
1½ cups (225g) plain (all-purpose) flour
80g (2½ ounces) cold butter, chopped
⅓ cup (80g) sour cream
1 egg yolk

1   Make sour cream pastry.
2   Meanwhile, heat oil in large saucepan, cook
fennel, celery and leek until softened. Add chicken
and garlic; cook, stirring, until chicken changes
colour. Add flour; cook, stirring, until mixture
thickens and bubbles. Gradually add combined
stock and cream; stir until mixture boils and
thickens. Reduce heat, simmer, uncovered, about
10 minutes or until thickened; season. Transfer to
1.5-litre (6-cup) ovenproof dish. Cool 20 minutes.
3   Preheat oven to 200°C/400°F.
4   Roll pastry between sheets of baking paper until
large enough to cover dish. Cover dish with pastry,
trim edges. Seal edges with fork; use pastry scraps
to decorate pie. Brush with egg white. Bake about
45 minutes or until browned.

SOUR CREAM PASTRY Process flour and butter
until crumbly. Add cream and yolk, process until
mixture comes together. Knead pastry on floured
surface until smooth, cover; refrigerate 30 minutes.

prep + cook time 1 hour 30 minutes (+ cooling)
serves 4
nutritional count per serving 47.4g total fat
(27g saturated fat); 3390kJ (811 cal);
49g carbohydrate; 45.1g protein; 5.8g fibre

note Sour cream pastry is lighter in texture but
richer in flavour than basic shortcrust pastry. It is
extremely easy to handle and may be used for
both savoury and sweet pies.

spanish chicken pie

170g (5½ ounces) cured chorizo sausage, sliced thinly
600g (1½ pounds) chicken thigh fillets, chopped coarsely
1 medium red onion (170g), chopped coarsely
2 celery stalks (300g), trimmed, chopped coarsely
250g (8 ounces) roasted red capsicum (bell pepper), chopped coarsely
1 small fennel bulb (200g), trimmed, sliced thinly
2 cloves garlic, crushed
½ teaspoon saffron threads
3 teaspoons mild paprika
¼ cup (70g) tomato paste
¾ cup (180ml) water
½ cup (60g) seeded black olives
2 medium potatoes (400g), unpeeled, sliced thinly

1 Heat large saucepan; cook chorizo, turning, until crisp. Remove from pan. Cook chicken, in batches, until browned all over. Remove from pan.
2 Add onion, celery, capsicum, fennel and garlic to pan; cook, stirring, until softened. Add saffron, paprika, paste and the water; bring to the boil. Return chicken and chorizo to pan. Reduce heat, simmer, uncovered, about 15 minutes or until chicken is cooked through and sauce thickens. Stir in olives. Transfer to 1.5-litre (6-cup) ovenproof dish.
3 Meanwhile, preheat oven to 220°C/425°F. Arrange potato slices, slightly overlapping, over chicken mixture. Bake, uncovered, about 45 minutes or until potatoes are tender.

prep + cook time 1 hour 30 minutes **serves** 4
nutritional count per serving 23.5g total fat (7.7g saturated fat); 2048kJ (490 cal); 28.9g carbohydrate; 38.1g protein; 5.8g fibre

chicken, bacon & blue cheese jalousie

1 tablespoon olive oil
3 bacon slices (240g), chopped coarsely
1 small leek (200g), sliced thinly
1 cup (160g) coarsely chopped barbecued chicken
125g (4 ounces) blue cheese
2 sheets puff pastry
1 egg, beaten lightly

1 Preheat oven to 220°C/425°F. Line oven tray with baking paper.
2 Heat half the oil in large frying pan; cook bacon until crisp. Drain on absorbent paper.
3 Heat remaining oil in same pan; cook leek, stirring, until tender. Combine leek in large bowl with bacon, chicken and cheese.

4 Cut each pastry sheet into two rectangles, one slightly larger than the other. Place smaller rectangles on tray. Top with chicken mixture, leaving a 1cm (½-inch) border. Brush edges lightly with egg.
5 Gently fold larger pastry rectangles in half lengthways. Cut through folded edge of pastry at 1cm (½-inch) intervals, leaving a 1cm (½-inch) border. Carefully unfold cut pastry strip, place over filling. Press edges of pastry together; brush lightly with egg.
6 Bake about 25 minutes or until browned.

prep + cook time 45 minutes **serves** 6
nutritional count per serving 29.3g total fat (7.9g saturated fat); 1864kJ (446 cal); 20.9g carbohydrate; 24.3g protein; 1.6g fibre

serving suggestion Serve with rocket (arugula) salad.

17

smoky paprika chicken tart

tip: You can use one quantity basic shortcrust pastry (page 4) instead of the store-bought pastry sheets.

1 teaspoon saffron threads
1 tablespoon boiling water
2 tablespoons olive oil
1 medium brown onion (150g), cut into thin wedges
1 medium red capsicum (bell pepper) (200g), chopped finely
2 cloves garlic, crushed
1 cured chorizo sausage (170g), sliced thinly
2 teaspoons smoked paprika
400g (12½ ounces) chicken thigh fillets, chopped coarsely
410g (13 ounces) canned diced tomatoes
2 tablespoons lemon juice
½ cup (125ml) water
2 sheets shortcrust pastry
2 slices sourdough bread (140g), torn into pieces
20g (¾ ounce) butter, melted
¼ cup (20g) finely grated manchego or parmesan cheese

1 Combine saffron and the boiling water in small heatproof bowl. Stand 5 minutes.
2 Heat oil in large frying pan; cook onion, capsicum, garlic and chorizo, stirring, until browned. Add paprika, cook, stirring, until fragrant. Add chicken, undrained tomatoes, juice, the water and saffron mixture. Simmer, uncovered, about 10 minutes or until thickened. Season to taste; cool.
3 Oil 24cm (9½-inch) round loose-based flan tin. Cut one pastry sheet in half. Join pieces to two sides of remaining pastry sheet. Lift pastry into tin, ease into side, trim edge; prick base all over with fork. Place on oven tray. Refrigerate 30 minutes.
4 Meanwhile, preheat oven to 200°C/400°F. Bake pastry case 15 minutes. Cool.
5 Spoon filling into pastry case. Combine bread and butter in bowl. Spoon over pie; sprinkle with cheese. Bake, uncovered, about 20 minutes or until browned. Stand pie 5 minutes before serving.

prep + cook time 1 hour 20 minutes
(+ cooling & refrigeration) **serves** 6
nutritional count per serving 41.3g total fat
(17.6g saturated fat); 2679kJ (641 cal);
41.6g carbohydrate; 24.8g protein; 3.5g fibre

chicken bastilla

1 tablespoon olive oil
800g (1½ pounds) chicken thigh fillets, chopped
2 medium red onions (340g), sliced thinly
2 cloves garlic, crushed
1 fresh long green chilli, chopped finely
½ teaspoon saffron threads
2 teaspoons ground coriander
1 teaspoon ground ginger
1½ cups (375ml) chicken stock
½ cup (40g) flaked almonds, roasted
3 eggs, beaten lightly
½ cup each coarsely chopped fresh coriander
   (cilantro) and fresh flat-leaf parsley
¼ cup coarsely chopped fresh mint
80g (2½ ounces) butter, melted
8 sheets fillo pastry
1 teaspoon icing (confectioners') sugar
½ teaspoon ground cinnamon

1 Heat half the oil in large frying pan; cook chicken, in batches, stirring occasionally, about 5 minutes or until browned. Remove from pan.
2 Heat remaining oil in pan; cook onion, stirring, until softened. Add garlic, chilli, and spices; cook, stirring, until fragrant. Add stock and chicken; bring to the boil. Reduce heat, simmer, uncovered, about 20 minutes or until liquid has almost evaporated. Transfer to bowl; cool 5 minutes. Stir in nuts, egg and herbs; season to taste.
3 Preheat oven to 200°C/400°F. Brush deep 20cm (8-inch) round cake pan with a little butter. Line an oven tray with baking paper.
4 Layer four sheets of pastry, brushing each with butter. Line cake pan with pastry, allowing edges to overhang. Repeat with remaining butter and pastry. Position pastry crossways over pastry in pan. Spoon chicken mixture into pan. Fold overlapping pastry over filling to enclose. Brush with butter.
5 Bake about 30 minutes or until browned. Turn pie onto tray. Bake about 15 minutes or until browned. Dust with sifted sugar and cinnamon.

prep + cook time 1 hour 45 minutes **serves** 6
nutritional count per serving 30.6g total fat (11.8g saturated fat); 1952kJ (467 cal); 14.6g carbohydrate; 33.1g protein; 2.4g fibre

cajun chicken and corn pies

1 tablespoon olive oil
1 medium brown onion (150g), chopped finely
1 trimmed corn cob (250g), kernels removed
2 cloves garlic, crushed
2 teaspoons cajun seasoning
400g (12½ ounces) chicken thigh fillets,
  chopped coarsely
2 tablespoons plain (all-purpose) flour
1 cup (250ml) chicken stock
2 tablespoons finely chopped fresh
  coriander (cilantro)
2 sheets shortcrust pastry
1 egg, beaten lightly
4 fresh small red thai (serrano) chillies

1 Heat oil in large frying pan; cook onion, corn
and garlic, stirring, until onion softens. Add
seasoning; cook, stirring, until fragrant. Add
chicken; cook, stirring, until chicken changes colour.
Add flour; cook, stirring, 1 minute. Gradually stir
in stock; stir over heat until mixture boils and
thickens; season, cool. Stir in coriander.

2 Preheat oven to 200°C/400°F. Oil four holes
of six-hole (¾-cup/180ml) texas muffin pan.
3 Cut four 13cm (5-inch) rounds from pastry;
press into pan holes. Divide chicken mixture
among pastry cases.
4 Cut four 9cm (3½-inch) rounds from pastry;
top chicken filling with pastry rounds. Press edges
firmly to seal; brush tops with egg. Insert a chilli
into each pie.
5 Bake pies about 25 minutes or until browned.
Stand pies in pan 5 minutes before serving.

prep + cook time 55 minutes (+ cooling) makes 4
nutritional count per serving 59.7g total fat
(27.6g saturated fat); 4322kJ (1034 cal);
88g carbohydrate; 34.7g protein; 6.1g fibre

tip One corn cob will give about 1 cup kernels. You
can substitute frozen or drained canned kernels.

chicken and leek strudel

1 tablespoon olive oil
1 medium brown onion (150g), chopped finely
1 medium leek (350g), white part only,
 sliced thinly
1 large carrot (180g), finely chopped
2 cloves garlic, crushed
500g (1 pound) chicken thigh fillets,
 chopped finely
2 tablespoons plain (all-purpose) flour
1¼ cups (310ml) pouring cream
8 sheets fillo pastry
80g (2½ ounces) butter, melted
⅓ cup (40g) ground almonds

1 Heat oil in large frying pan; cook onion, leek,
carrot and garlic, stirring, until carrot softens. Add
chicken; cook, stirring, until browned. Add flour;
cook, stirring, 1 minute. Gradually stir in cream;
cook, stirring, until mixture boils and thickens.
Season to taste. Cool.

2 Preheat oven to 200°C/400°F.
3 Line large oven tray with baking paper. Brush
one pastry sheet with melted butter; sprinkle with a
little of the almonds. Layer with remaining pastry,
butter and almonds, ending with a pastry sheet.
4 Spoon chicken mixture along one long side
of pastry, leaving a 5cm (2-inch) border on each
side. Roll to enclose filling, fold in sides, roll up.
Transfer roll to tray; brush with butter. Bake about
25 minutes or until browned. Stand strudel on tray
5 minutes before serving.

prep + cook time 1 hour (+ cooling & standing)
serves 8
nutritional count per serving 32.6g total fat
(16.8g saturated fat); 1739kJ (416 cal);
14.3g carbohydrate; 16.1g protein; 2.6g fibre

tip: It is fine to use just 1 x 300ml carton of cream
for this recipe.

thai green curry chicken pies

1 tablespoon vegetable oil
500g (1 pound) chicken thigh fillets,
  chopped coarsely
1 medium potato (200g), chopped coarsely
1 tablespoon thai green curry paste
⅔ cup (160ml) light coconut milk
⅔ cup (160ml) water
1 tablespoon lime juice
100g (3 ounces) green beans, trimmed,
  chopped coarsely
2 tablespoons finely chopped fresh
  coriander (cilantro)
2 sheets shortcrust pastry
1 egg, beaten lightly

1 Heat oil in large saucepan; cook chicken,
stirring, until browned all over. Add potato and
paste, cook, stirring, until fragrant. Add coconut
milk, the water and juice; bring to the boil. Reduce
heat, simmer, uncovered, about 10 minutes or until
potato is tender and sauce is thick. Remove from
heat, stir in beans and coriander; season to taste.
Cool 30 minutes.
2 Preheat oven to 200°C/400°F. Oil four holes
of six-hole (¾-cup/180ml) texas muffin pan. Cut
four 13cm (5-inch) rounds and four 9cm (3½-inch)
rounds from pastry. Line base and side of holes
with larger rounds. Divide chicken mixture among
pastry cases.
3 Brush one side of smaller rounds with egg.
Place egg side down over filling. Press edges to
seal; brush tops with egg. Use pastry scraps to
decorate pies. Bake pies about 45 minutes or
until browned lightly.

prep + cook time 1 hour 25 minutes makes 4
nutritional count per serving 41.2g total fat
(18.4g saturated fat); 2830kJ (677 cal);
43.7g carbohydrate; 32.2g protein; 3.1g fibre

chicken, mushroom and gnocchi pie

1 tablespoon olive oil
500g (1 pound) chicken thigh fillets,
  chopped coarsely
30g (1 ounce) butter
1 medium brown onion (150g), chopped finely
2 cloves garlic, sliced thinly
300g (9½ ounces) mixed mushrooms, sliced thinly
3 sprigs fresh thyme
1 tablespoon plain (all-purpose) flour
⅓ cup (80ml) dry white wine
½ cup (125ml) chicken stock
⅓ cup (80ml) pouring cream
¼ cup coarsely chopped fresh flat-leaf parsley
500g (1 pound) gnocchi
½ cup (40g) finely grated parmesan cheese

1 Preheat oven to 220°C/425°F. Oil 1.5-litre (6-cup)
ovenproof dish.
2 Heat oil in large frying pan; cook chicken until
browned all over. Remove from pan.
3 Heat butter in same pan; cook onion, garlic,
mushrooms and thyme until vegetables are tender.
Add flour; cook, stirring, until mixture bubbles and
thickens. Stir in wine, stock, cream and chicken.
Bring to the boil, stirring until mixture boils and
thickens slightly. Discard thyme. Stir in parsley;
season to taste. Pour mixture into dish.
4 Meanwhile, cook gnocchi in large saucepan of
boiling salted water about 3 minutes or until
gnocchi float. Drain well.
5 Spoon gnocchi over filling. Sprinkle with cheese.
Bake uncovered, about 20 minutes or until
browned lightly.

prep + cook time 55 minutes **serves** 4
nutritional count per serving 32g total fat
(15g saturated fat); 2629kJ (629 cal);
42.7g carbohydrate; 36.8g protein; 5.6g fibre

seafood pies

tomato and saffron fish pies

1 cup (250ml) fish stock
1 bay leaf
pinch saffron threads
1 tablespoon olive oil
1 medium red onion (170g), chopped finely
3 cloves garlic, crushed
1 long fresh red chilli, sliced thinly
1 medium red capsicum (bell pepper) (200g),
  chopped coarsely
410g (13 ounces) canned crushed tomatoes
650g (1¼ pounds) firm white fish fillets,
  chopped coarsely
2 tablespoons coarsely chopped fresh
  flat-leaf parsley
1 thin french bread stick, sliced thickly
cooking-oil spray

1 Combine stock, bay leaf and saffron in medium saucepan. Bring to the boil; simmer, covered, 5 minutes.
2 Preheat oven to 220°C/425°F. Oil six 1-cup (250ml) ovenproof dishes.
3 Meanwhile, heat oil in large saucepan; cook onion, garlic, chilli and capsicum, stirring, until vegetables are tender. Add undrained tomatoes and hot stock mixture. Bring to the boil; simmer, uncovered, about 10 minutes or until thickened slightly. Remove from heat, stir in fish and parsley; season. Divide mixture among dishes; place on oven tray. Top each dish with two or three slices of bread. Spray bread with oil.
4 Bake uncovered, about 15 minutes or until bread is crisp.

prep + cook time 40 minutes makes 6
nutritional count per serving 7g total fat
(1.4g saturated fat); 1041kJ (249 cal);
18.5g carbohydrate; 26.3g protein; 2.8g fibre

note We used ling in this recipe, but any white fish fillet will be fine.

greek prawn pies

1 tablespoon olive oil
1 medium brown onion (150g), chopped finely
2 cloves garlic, crushed
3 teaspoons plain (all-purpose) flour
¼ cup (60ml) dry white wine
410g (13 ounces) canned diced tomatoes
750g (1½ pounds) uncooked medium king prawns
  (shrimp), shelled, deveined
2 tablespoons finely chopped fresh
  flat-leaf parsley
12 sheets fillo pastry
60g (2 ounces) butter, melted
50g (1½ ounces) fetta cheese, crumbled

1 Heat oil in large frying pan; cook onion and garlic, stirring, until onion softens. Add flour, cook; stirring 1 minute. Add wine and undrained tomatoes; bring to the boil, stirring. Reduce heat; simmer, uncovered, about 3 minutes or until sauce thickens slightly. Add prawns and parsley; cook 1 minute. Season to taste. Cool.
2 Preheat oven to 200°C/400°F. Oil six-hole (¾-cup/180ml) texas muffin pan.
3 Layer two sheets of pastry, brushing each with butter. Fold in thirds to enclose buttered side. Brush with butter; fold in half, forming a square; brush with butter. Gently press into pan hole. Repeat with remaining pastry and butter.
4 Bake pastry cases about 5 minutes or until browned lightly.
5 Divide prawn mixture among pastry cases; top with cheese. Bake about 10 minutes or until browned lightly. Stand 5 minutes before serving.

prep + cook time 45 minutes (+ cooling) **makes** 6
nutritional count per serving 14.4g total fat
(7.3g saturated fat); 1254kJ (300 cal);
21.3g carbohydrate; 18.5g protein; 2.2g fibre

serving suggestion Serve with lemon wedges.

smoked cod and cheddar pie

500g (1 pound) smoked cod
2⅓ cups (580ml) milk
1 bay leaf
30g (1 ounce) butter
1 medium brown onion (150g), chopped finely
200g (6½ ounces) speck, chopped finely
2 tablespoons plain (all-purpose) flour
⅓ cup (80ml) dry white wine
½ cup (60g) coarsely grated cheddar cheese
2 tablespoons finely chopped fresh chives
400g (12½ ounces) white fish fillets,
  chopped coarsely
1 sheet puff pastry
1 egg, beaten lightly

1 Preheat oven to 220°C/ 425°F. Oil 1.5-litre
(6-cup) ovenproof dish.
2 Place cod in large saucepan with 1⅓ cups
(330ml) of the milk and bay leaf. Bring to the boil;
simmer, uncovered, 5 minutes. Drain; discard milk
and bay leaf. Flake fish; discard skin and bones.
3 Heat butter in same pan; cook onion and speck,
stirring, until onion is soft. Add flour; cook, stirring,
until mixture bubbles and thickens. Gradually add
wine; simmer, uncovered, 1 minute. Gradually stir
in remaining milk; simmer, uncovered, 1 minute;
remove from heat. Stir in cheese, chives and all
fish; season.
4 Spoon mixture into dish. Top with pastry,
trimming to fit. Use pastry scraps to decorate pie.
Brush pastry with egg. Bake about 20 minutes or
until browned.

prep + cook time 40 minutes **serves** 4
nutritional count per serving 38.2g total fat
(15.9g saturated fat); 3122kJ (747 cal);
28.3g carbohydrate; 69.2g protein; 1.3g fibre

tip We used ling in this recipe, but any firm white
fish fillet will be fine.

creamy bacon and fish pie with potato topping

60g (2 ounces) butter
2 rindless bacon slices (160g), sliced thinly
1 medium leek (350g), trimmed, sliced thinly
2 tablespoons plain (all-purpose) flour
¾ cup (180ml) chicken stock
1 cup (250ml) pouring cream
3 cups (250g) broccoli florets
650g (1¼ pounds) skinless white fish fillets,
  chopped coarsely
1 medium potato (200g), sliced thinly
¼ cup (30g) coarsely grated cheddar cheese

1 Preheat oven to 220°C/425°F. Oil 1.5-litre (6-cup) ovenproof dish.
2 Melt butter in large saucepan; cook bacon and leek, stirring, until leek is soft. Add flour; cook, stirring, until mixture bubbles and thickens. Gradually stir in stock, cream and broccoli. Stir over heat until mixture boils and thickens. Add fish; stir until heated through. Season.
3 Spoon mixture into dish. Top with potato, sprinkle with cheese.
4 Bake uncovered, about 25 minutes or until browned lightly.

prep + cook time 45 minutes (+ cooling) **serves** 4
nutritional count per serving 45.2g total fat
(27.3g saturated fat); 2784kJ (666 cal);
14.3g carbohydrate; 49.2g protein; 5g fibre

note We used blue eye in this recipe, but any white fish fillet will be fine.

balti curry prawn and roti pies

2 tablespoons vegetable oil
1 medium brown onion (150g), chopped coarsely
1cm (½-inch) piece fresh ginger (5g), grated
⅓ cup (100g) balti curry paste
¾ cup (180ml) chicken stock
5 large egg (plum) tomatoes (450g),
  chopped coarsely
800g (1½ pounds) uncooked prawns (shrimp),
  shelled, deveined
½ cup (60g) frozen peas
¼ cup coarsely chopped fresh coriander (cilantro)
4 roti bread

1 Preheat oven to 220°C/425°F. Oil four 1¼-cup (310ml) ovenproof dishes.
2 Heat half the oil in large frying pan; cook onion and ginger; stirring, until onion softens. Add paste; cook, stirring, until fragrant. Add stock and tomato; bring to the boil, simmer, uncovered, about 5 minutes or until tomato is tender. Remove from heat. Stir in prawns, peas and coriander; season. Spoon mixture into dishes.
3 Cut two 9cm (3½-inch) rounds from each roti bread. Place over filling. Brush with remaining oil. Bake pies, uncovered, about 15 minutes or until browned and crisp.

prep + cook time 45 minutes **makes** 4
nutritional count per serving 20.6g total fat (2.9g saturated fat); 1940kJ (464 cal); 35.9g carbohydrate; 29.6g protein; 8.3g fibre

fish pies with potato scales topping

2 medium potatoes (400g)
40g (1½ ounces) butter
1 small leek (200g), sliced thinly
¼ cup (35g) plain (all-purpose) flour
1 cup (250ml) pouring cream
500g (1 pound) thick white boneless fish fillets, chopped coarsely
2 tablespoons finely chopped fresh flat-leaf parsley
20g (¾ ounce) butter, melted, extra

SHORTCRUST PASTRY
1½ cups (225g) plain (all-purpose) flour
80g (2½ ounces) butter
1 egg
2 tablespoons iced water, approximately

1 Make shortcrust pastry.
2 Boil or steam whole unpeeled potatoes about 20 minutes or until tender. Drain; cool. Peel potatoes; slice thinly.
3 Meanwhile, melt butter in medium saucepan; cook leek, stirring, until soft. Add flour; cook, stirring, 1 minute. Gradually stir in cream; stir over heat until mixture boils and thickens. Season to taste, cool. Stir in fish and parsley.
4 Preheat oven to 200°C/400°F. Oil six 1-cup (250ml) ovenproof dishes. Roll pastry between sheets of baking paper until large enough to line dishes. Lift pastry into dishes, ease into bases and sides; trim edges. Prick bases well; place dishes on oven tray. Refrigerate 30 minutes.
5 Bake pastry cases 15 minutes. Cool.
6 Spoon fish mixture into pastry cases. Top with slightly overlapping potato slices; brush with extra butter. Bake about 20 minutes or until browned. Stand pies 5 minutes before serving.

SHORTCRUST PASTRY Process flour and butter until crumbly. Add egg and most of the water; process until ingredients just come together. Knead pastry on floured surface until smooth, enclose with plastic wrap; refrigerate 30 minutes.

prep + cook time 1 hour 15 minutes (+ refrigeration & cooling) makes 6
nutritional count per serving 38g total fat (23.7g saturated fat); 2475kJ (592 cal); 37g carbohydrate; 24.9g protein; 2.7g fibre

serving suggestion Serve with lemon wedges.
tip We used blue eye in this recipe, but any firm white fish fillet will be fine.

smoked salmon vol-au-vents

2 sheets puff pastry
1 egg, beaten lightly
125g (4 ounces) smoked salmon, chopped finely
1 lebanese cucumber (130g), seeded, chopped finely
½ small red onion (50g), chopped finely
1 tablespoon baby capers, chopped finely
1 tablespoon finely chopped fresh dill
1 tablespoon lime juice
2 tablespoons sour cream

1 Preheat oven to 200°C/400°F. Line an oven tray with baking paper.
2 Cut 12 x 8cm (3¼-inch) rounds from pastry; place on oven tray. Brush edges of pastry rounds with egg. Cut out 5.5cm (3½-inch) rounds from centre of six of the rounds; place rings onto rounds. Brush with egg.
3 Bake pastry about 12 minutes or until browned lightly. Gently press centre of cases with a tea towel to flatten.
4 Combine salmon, cucumber, onion, capers, dill and juice in medium bowl; season to taste. Spoon into pastry cases. Top with sour cream.

prep + cook time 30 minutes **makes** 6
nutritional count per serving 23.5g total fat (3.6g saturated fat); 1597kJ (382 cal); 31.1g carbohydrate; 10.9g protein; 1.4g fibre

thai-flavoured scallop pies

12 wonton or gow gee wrappers
¼ cup (60ml) vegetable oil
3 shallots (75g), chopped finely
1 fresh small red thai (serrano) chilli,
  chopped finely
⅔ cup (160ml) coconut milk
1 tablespoon fish sauce
1 tablespoon lime juice
3 teaspoons light brown sugar
3 fresh kaffir lime leaves, shredded finely
3 teaspoons cornflour (cornstarch)
1 tablespoon water
500g (1 pound) scallops, without roe,
  chopped coarsely
¼ cup fresh coriander (cilantro) leaves
1 fresh small red thai (serrano) chilli, sliced
  thinly, extra

1 Preheat oven to 200°C/400°F. Oil 12-hole
(⅓-cup/80ml) muffin pan.
2 Brush wrappers with half the oil; press into pan
holes. Bake about 10 minutes or until crisp. Stand
in pan 5 minutes. Transfer to a wire rack; cool.
3 Heat remaining oil in large frying pan; cook
shallot and chilli, stirring, until softened. Add
coconut milk, sauce, juice, sugar and lime leaves.
Cook, stirring, until fragrant. Bring to the boil. Stir
in blended cornflour and the water; cook, stirring,
until sauce boils and thickens.
4 Add scallops; simmer, uncovered, until almost
cooked through. Season. Spoon scallop mixture
into pie shells. Top with coriander and extra chilli.

prep + cook time 30 minutes makes 12
nutritional count per serving 7.8g total fat
(3.1g saturated fat); 485kJ (116 cal);
5.5g carbohydrate; 5.9g protein; 0.5g fibre

salmon coulibiac

1 cup (150g) cooked white rice
2 green onions (scallions), sliced thinly
2 hard-boiled eggs, mashed
1 tablespoon mayonnaise
1 tablespoon finely chopped fresh dill
210g (6½ ounces) canned red salmon, drained
1 egg, beaten lightly

SHORTCRUST PASTRY
2 cups (300g) plain (all-purpose) flour
250g (8 ounces) cold butter, chopped
1 teaspoon finely grated lemon rind
¼ cup (60ml) iced water, approximately

1   Make shortcrust pastry.
2   Preheat oven to 220°C/425°F. Heat large oven tray.
3   Combine rice and onion in small bowl. Combine egg, mayonnaise and dill in small bowl; season. Remove skin and bones from salmon; mash.
4   Cut one third of pasty from block; refrigerate. Roll remaining pastry between sheets of baking paper until 20cm x 26cm (8 inches x 10½ inches).
5   Spoon rice mixture over pastry, leaving a 3cm (1¼-inch) border. Top with salmon then egg mixture.
6   Roll refrigerated pastry until 24cm x 29cm (9½ inches x 11½ inches). Mark a rectangle 2cm (¾ inch) in from edge of pastry. Put pastry over filling, pressing edges together. Mark lines across pastry. Brush with egg.
7   Bake on hot tray about 20 minutes or until browned. Stand 5 minutes.

SHORTCRUST PASTRY Pulse flour, butter and rind five times in processor; turn onto flat surface. Knead in enough of the water until pastry just comes together. Enclose in plastic wrap; refrigerate 30 minutes.

prep + cook time 1 hour (+ refrigeration) **serves** 6
nutritional count per serving 41.8g total fat (24.5g saturated fat); 2567kJ (614 cal); 43.7g carbohydrate; 15.7g protein; 2.1g fibre

tuna, pasta and char-grilled vegetable pie

250g (8 ounces) penne pasta
3 medium zucchini (360g), sliced thinly
1 medium red capsicum (bell pepper)
  (200g), quartered
3 baby eggplants (180g), sliced thinly
2 tablespoons olive oil
1 medium brown onion (150g), chopped finely
2 cloves garlic, crushed
410g (13 ounces) canned crushed tomatoes
425g (13½ ounces) canned tuna in oil,
  drained, flaked
2 tablespoons finely chopped fresh basil
4 eggs, beaten lightly
1 cup (60g) coarse ciabatta breadcrumbs
¼ cup (20g) pizza cheese

1 Cook pasta in medium saucepan of boiling
water, uncovered, until tender; drain.
2 Meanwhile, combine zucchini, capsicum and
eggplant in large bowl with half the oil; season.
Cook vegetables on heated oiled grill plate (or
grill, barbecue or grill pan) until browned both
sides and tender. Cut into small pieces.
3 Preheat oven to 200°C/400°F. Oil 22cm (9-inch)
springform tin; line base and side with baking paper.
Stand tin on oven tray.
4 Heat remaining oil in large saucepan; cook
onion and garlic, stirring, until tender. Add
undrained tomatoes; bring to the boil. Simmer,
uncovered, 2 minutes. Remove from heat, stir in
tuna, basil, vegetables and pasta; season to taste.
Cool slightly; stir in eggs. Pour mixture into tin.
Sprinkle with breadcrumbs and cheese.
5 Bake pie about 50 minutes or until browned
and set. Stand 20 minutes before serving.

prep + cook time 1 hour 25 minutes (+ standing)
serves 8
nutritional count per serving 14.5g total fat
(2.8g saturated fat); 1425kJ (341 cal);
29.8g carbohydrate; 20.7g protein; 3.7g fibre

tip Pie is best left to cool completely before slicing.

chunky pork and fennel pie

1kg (2 pounds) diced pork neck
⅓ cup (50g) plain (all-purpose) flour
2 tablespoons olive oil
1 large brown onion (200g), chopped coarsely
1 large carrot (180g), chopped coarsely
1 stick celery (150g), trimmed, chopped coarsely
1 large fennel bulb (550g), sliced thinly
2 cloves garlic, crushed
2 teaspoons chopped fresh thyme
1⅓ cups (330ml) chicken stock
2 tablespoons chopped fennel tops
1 tablespoon wholegrain mustard
1 egg, beaten lightly
¼ teaspoon fennel seeds

FENNEL PASTRY
3 cups (450g) plain (all-purpose) flour
1 teaspoon fennel seeds
200g (6½ ounces) butter, chopped
2 eggs
¼ cup (60ml) iced water, approximately

1 Toss pork in flour; shake away excess. Heat oil in large saucepan; cook pork, in batches, until browned; remove from pan.
2 Add onion, carrot, celery and fennel to pan; cook, stirring, until softened. Add garlic and thyme; cook, stirring, until fragrant. Return pork to pan with stock; bring to the boil. Simmer, covered, 1½ hours. Simmer, uncovered, about 20 minutes or until mixture is slightly thickened. Stir in fennel tops and mustard; season to taste, cool.
3 Meanwhile, make fennel pastry.
4 Preheat oven to 180°C/350°F. Oil deep 24cm (9½-inch) pie dish (1.5-litre/6-cups).
5 Roll half the pastry between sheets of baking paper until large enough to line dish. Press pastry into side; trim edge. Prick base with fork. Cover pastry with baking paper, fill with dried beans or rice. Bake 15 minutes. Remove paper and beans, bake further 10 minutes or until browned. Cool.
6 Spoon pork mixture into pastry case. Brush edge of pastry with egg. Roll remaining pastry until large enough to cover top of dish, place over filling; pinch edges together, trim. Brush with egg; sprinkle with seeds. Cut several steam holes in pastry.
7 Place pie on oven tray; bake about 30 minutes or until browned.

FENNEL PASTRY Process flour, seeds and butter until crumbly. Add eggs and enough of the water to make ingredients just come together. Knead pastry on floured surface until smooth, enclose with plastic wrap; refrigerate 30 minutes.

prep + cook time 3 hours 30 minutes (+ refrigeration & cooling) serves 6
nutritional count per serving 43.8g total fat (22.3g saturated fat); 3632kJ (869 cal); 66.1g carbohydrate; 50.1g protein; 6.3g fibre

serving suggestion Serve with a green salad.

chunky beef and mushroom pies

600g (1¼ pounds) beef chuck steak,
  chopped coarsely
2 tablespoons plain (all-purpose) flour
2 tablespoons olive oil
1 small brown onion (80g), chopped finely
2 cloves garlic, crushed
125g (4 ounces) mushrooms, chopped coarsely
410g (13 ounces) canned crushed tomatoes
¾ cup (180ml) beef stock
2 tablespoons tomato paste
2 tablespoons worcestershire sauce
3 sheets shortcrust pastry
2 sheets puff pastry
1 egg, beaten lightly

TOMATO SAUCE
1 tablespoon olive oil
1 medium brown onion (150g), chopped coarsely
2 tablespoons light brown sugar
800g (1½ pounds) canned crushed tomatoes
1 teaspoon ground allspice
2 tablespoons tomato paste
¼ cup (60ml) white wine vinegar

1 Coat beef in flour; shake off excess. Heat half the oil in large saucepan; cook beef, in batches, until browned. Remove from pan.
2 Heat remaining oil in same pan; cook onion, garlic and mushrooms, stirring, until vegetables soften. Return beef to pan with undrained tomatoes, stock, paste and sauce; bring to the boil. Reduce heat; simmer, covered, 1 hour. Uncover; simmer about 15 minutes or until thickened slightly. Season to taste; cool.
3 Meanwhile, make tomato sauce.
4 Oil six ⅔-cup (160ml) pie tins; place on oven tray. Cut six 13cm (5¼-inch) rounds from shortcrust pastry. Ease pastry into tins, press into base and sides; trim edges. Refrigerate 30 minutes.
5 Preheat oven to 200°C/400°F.
6 Line pastry with baking paper; fill with dried beans or rice. Bake 10 minutes; remove paper and beans. Bake further 5 minutes; cool.
7 Cut six 11cm (4½-inch) rounds from puff pastry. Fill pastry cases with beef filling; brush edges with egg. Top with puff pastry rounds; press edges to seal. Brush tops with egg; cut steam holes in tops. Bake about 25 minutes or until browned lightly. Serve pies with tomato sauce.

TOMATO SAUCE Heat oil in medium saucepan; cook onion, stirring, until soft. Add sugar, undrained tomatoes and allspice; bring to the boil. Reduce heat; simmer, uncovered, stirring occasionally, about 30 minutes or until mixture thickens. Stir in paste and vinegar; cook, uncovered, 5 minutes. Blend or process sauce until smooth. Push through fine sieve into medium bowl; discard solids. Cool.

prep + cook time 2 hours (+ refrigeration)
makes 6
nutritional count per pie (with sauce) 53.8g total fat (17.1g saturated fat); 3992kJ (955 cal); 77.9g carbohydrate; 36.6g protein; 7.5g fibre

beef and lentil pies with kumara mash

1 tablespoon olive oil
1 medium brown onion (150g), chopped finely
2 cloves garlic, crushed
500g (1 pound) minced (ground) beef
1 tablespoon ground cumin
2 teaspoons ground coriander
2 tablespoons tomato paste
1 cup (250ml) beef stock
400g (12½ ounces) canned brown lentils,
 rinsed, drained
⅓ cup coarsely chopped fresh coriander (cilantro)
1 medium kumara (orange sweet potato) (400g),
 chopped coarsely
1 medium potato (200g), chopped coarsely
20g (¾ ounce) butter
2 tablespoons milk
½ teaspoon cumin seeds

1 Preheat oven to 220°C/425°F.
2 Heat oil in large saucepan; cook onion and
garlic, stirring, until onion softens. Add beef;
cook, stirring, until browned. Add spices; cook,
stirring, until fragrant. Add paste, stock and
lentils. Bring to the boil; simmer, uncovered,
about 10 minutes or until thickened slightly.
Stir in coriander; season to taste.
3 Meanwhile, boil, steam or microwave kumara
and potato until tender; drain. Mash vegetables in
large bowl with butter and milk until smooth;
season to taste.
4 Spoon mixture into four 1¼-cup (310ml)
ovenproof dishes. Top with mash. Sprinkle with seeds.
5 Bake pies about 20 minutes or until browned.

prep + cook time 55 minutes makes 4
nutritional count per serving 19g total fat
(8.3g saturated fat); 1731kJ (414cal);
25.7g carbohydrate; 32.8g protein; 5.1g fibre

chilli beef pies with cornbread topping

1 tablespoon olive oil
1 medium brown onion (150g), chopped finely
350g (11 ounces) minced (ground) beef
1½ teaspoons mexican chilli powder
1 tablespoon plain (all-purpose) flour
375g (12 ounces) bottled chunky mild salsa
½ cup (125ml) chicken stock
2 sheets shortcrust pastry
½ cup (85g) polenta
½ cup (75g) self-raising flour
½ cup (60g) coarsely grated cheddar cheese
⅔ cup (160ml) buttermilk
1 egg, beaten lightly
20g (¾ ounce) butter, melted
¼ cup (30g) coarsely grated cheddar cheese

1 Heat oil in large frying pan; cook onion, stirring, until soft. Add beef; cook, stirring, until browned. Add chilli powder; cook, stirring, until fragrant. Stir in flour, salsa and stock; bring to the boil, stirring; simmer, uncovered, 10 minutes. Season; cool.
2 Preheat oven to 200°C/400°F. Oil four 1-cup (250ml) round pie tins. Cut four 16cm (6½-inch) rounds from pastry. Lift pastry into tins, ease into bases and sides, trim edges; prick bases with fork. Refrigerate 20 minutes. Place pie tins on oven tray; bake 10 minutes. Cool.
3 Divide beef mixture among pastry cases. Combine polenta, flour and cheese in medium bowl. Stir in combined buttermilk, egg and butter. Spoon polenta mixture onto pies; sprinkle the tops with cheese.
4 Stand tins on oven tray, bake about 20 minutes or until browned lightly. Stand pies 5 minutes before serving.

prep + cook time 1 hour 20 minutes
(+ cooling & refrigeration) **makes** 4
nutritional count per serving 48.3g total fat
(23.9g saturated fat); 3695kJ (884 cal);
72.9g carbohydrate; 37.6g protein; 4.7g fibre

argentinean empanadas

2 tablespoons olive oil
750g (1½ pounds) beef chuck steak,
  chopped coarsely
1 medium brown onion (150g), chopped finely
2 teaspoons plain (all-purpose) flour
2 teaspoons ground cumin
1 teaspoon each ground coriander and
  sweet paprika
2 cups (500ml) beef stock
4 sheets shortcrust pastry
4 large green olives, seeded, sliced thinly
2 hard-boiled eggs, chopped coarsely
1 egg, beaten lightly
340g (11 ounces) bottled roasted capsicum strips
  (bell pepper)

1   Heat half the oil in large saucepan; cook beef, in
batches, until browned. Remove from pan.
2   Heat remaining oil in same pan; cook onion,
stirring, until softened. Add flour and spices;
cook, stirring, 1 minute. Gradually stir in stock.
Return beef to pan; bring to the boil. Simmer,
covered, over low heat for 2 hours. Season to
taste; cool.

3   Preheat oven to 220°C/425°F. Oil and line
oven tray.
4   Cut eight 14cm (5½-inch) rounds from pastry.
Divide mixture among rounds. Top with olive and
hard-boiled egg; seal pastry over filling. Pinch
pastry edges together; place on oven tray. Brush
with beaten egg. Bake about 25 minutes or until
browned. Stand empanadas 5 minutes before serving.
5   Meanwhile, blend or process capsicum until
smooth. Serve with empanadas.

prep + cook time 3 hours **makes** 8
nutritional count per serving 36.7g total fat
(15.7g saturated fat); 2587kJ (619 cal);
25.7g carbohydrate; 32.8g protein; 5.1g fibre

asian beef and eggplant cups

1 tablespoon peanut oil
4 cloves garlic, sliced thinly
4cm (1½-inch) piece ginger (20g), grated
1 fresh long red chilli, halved, sliced thinly
1 medium eggplant (300g), chopped finely
500g (1 pound) minced (ground) beef
¼ cup (70g) plum sauce
2 tablespoons dark soy sauce
2 green onions (scallions), sliced thinly
18 sheets spring roll pastry
cooking-oil spray

1 Heat oil in large saucepan; cook garlic, ginger, chilli and eggplant, stirring, until tender. Add beef, cook, stirring, until browned.
2 Add sauces and onion; bring to the boil, simmer, uncovered, 5 minutes. Cool.

3 Meanwhile, preheat oven to 200°C/400°F. Oil six-hole (¾-cup/180ml) texas muffin pan.
4 Cut each pastry sheet into 14cm (5½-inch) squares. Layer 3 squares, spraying each with oil, overlapping to make a star pattern. Place in pan hole; spray with oil. Repeat with remaining pastry. Spoon filling into cases.
5 Bake about 20 minutes or until browned.

prep + cook time 50 minutes (+ cooling) **makes** 6
nutritional count per serving 10.7g total fat (3.4g saturated fat); 1129kJ (270 cal); 22.7g carbohydrate; 19.7g protein; 2.4g fibre

beef shiraz pies

750g (1½ pounds) beef chuck steak,
  chopped coarsely
2 tablespoons plain (all-purpose) flour
¼ cup (60ml) olive oil
1 medium brown onion (150g), chopped finely
1 medium carrot (120g), chopped finely
2 stalks celery (300g), trimmed, chopped finely
2 cloves garlic, crushed
½ cup (125ml) dry red wine
½ cup (125ml) beef stock
410g (13 ounces) canned diced tomatoes
2 tablespoons fresh thyme leaves
1 egg, beaten lightly

SOUR CREAM PASTRY
2¼ cups (335g) plain (all-purpose) flour
125g (4 ounces) cold butter, chopped coarsely
½ cup (120g) sour cream

1 Preheat oven to 180°C/350°F. Oil six-hole
(¾-cup/180ml) texas muffin pan.
2 Toss beef in flour, shake away excess. Heat half
the oil in large frying pan; cook beef, in batches,
until browned. Transfer beef to 3-litre (12-cup)
ovenproof dish.
3 Heat remaining oil in same pan; cook onion,
carrot, celery and garlic, stirring, until softened.
Add wine; bring to the boil. Stir in stock, undrained
tomatoes and thyme; bring to the boil. Pour over
beef. Cook, covered, 2 hours. Season to taste; cool.
4 Meanwhile, make sour cream pastry.
5 Roll two-thirds of the pastry between sheets of
baking paper until large enough to cut six 13cm
(5-inch) rounds; press pastry into pan holes. Brush
edges with egg. Divide beef mixture among
pastry cases.
6 Cut six 9cm (3½-inch) rounds from remaining
pastry; place pastry over filling. Press edges firmly
to seal; brush tops with egg. Cut a small slit in top
of each pie.
7 Bake pies about 30 minutes or until browned.
Stand pies 5 minutes before serving.

SOUR CREAM PASTRY Process flour and butter
until crumbly. Add sour cream; process until
ingredients barely cling together. Knead dough on
floured surface until smooth. Enclose in plastic
wrap; refrigerate 30 minutes.

prep + cook time 3 hours
(+ cooling & refrigeration) makes 6
nutritional count per serving 45.7g total fat
(21.6g saturated fat); 3202kJ (766 cal);
46.5g carbohydrate; 37.1g protein; 4.4g fibre

notes Sour cream pastry is lighter in texture but
richer in flavour than basic shortcrust pastry. It is
extremely easy to handle and may be used for both
savoury and sweet pies.
We used shiraz for this recipe, but you can use any
red wine you like.

veal and tomato pies with gremolata

800g (1½ pounds) diced veal
2 tablespoons plain (all-purpose) flour
2 tablespoons olive oil
1 large brown onion (200g), sliced thinly
2 cloves garlic, crushed
½ cup (125ml) dry white wine
¾ cup (180ml) chicken stock
410g (13 ounces) canned diced tomatoes
2 tablespoons tomato paste
2 dried bay leaves
2 sheets shortcrust pastry
1 egg, beaten lightly
2 teaspoons finely grated lemon rind
¼ cup finely chopped fresh flat-leaf parsley
2 cloves garlic, crushed, extra

1   Coat veal in flour; shake off excess. Heat half the oil in large saucepan; cook veal, in batches, until browned. Remove from pan.
2   Heat remaining oil in same pan; cook onion and garlic, stirring, until onion softens. Add wine; boil, uncovered, stirring, until liquid evaporates. Return veal to pan with stock, undrained tomatoes, paste and bay leaves; bring to the boil. Reduce heat; simmer, covered, 1 hour. Uncover; simmer, about 45 minutes or until veal is tender and mixture is thick. Discard bay leaves. Season to taste; cool.
3   Preheat oven to 200°C/400°F.
4   Spoon veal mixture into four 1-cup (250ml) ovenproof dishes. Cut four 14cm (5½-inch) rounds from pastry. Lift pastry over dishes, pressing edges. Cut a slit in tops; brush with egg. Bake about 20 minutes. Serve with combined rind, parsley and extra garlic.

prep + cook time 2 hours
(+ refrigeration & cooling) **serves** 4
nutritional count per serving 25g total fat (11.7g saturated fat); 2153kJ (515 cal); 32.4g carbohydrate; 38.4g protein; 3.3g fibre

tip You can use one quantity parmesan pastry (page 81) or one quantity basic shortcrust pastry (page 4) instead of the store-bought pastry sheets.

cottage pie

2 tablespoons olive oil
1 medium brown onion (150g), chopped finely
1 medium carrot (120g), chopped finely
500g (1 pound) minced (ground) beef
2 tablespoons plain (all-purpose) flour
¾ cup (180ml) beef stock
2 tablespoons tomato sauce (ketchup)
1 tablespoon worcestershire sauce
2 tablespoons finely chopped parsley
2 sheets shortcrust pastry
600g (1¼ pounds) potatoes, peeled,
  chopped coarsely
40g (1½ ounces) butter
½ cup (125ml) hot milk
⅓ cup (40g) coarsely grated cheddar cheese

1 Heat oil in large frying pan; cook onion and
carrot, stirring, until soft. Add beef, cook, stirring,
until beef changes colour. Add flour; cook, stirring,
1 minute. Gradually stir in combined stock and
sauces; stir over heat until mixture boils and
thickens. Simmer, uncovered, 10 minutes; stir in
parsley, season to taste, cool.
2 Preheat oven to 200°C/400°F. Oil 24cm (9½-inch)
loose-based flan tin. Cut one sheet of pastry in half.
Join pieces to two sides of remaining pastry sheet.
Lift pastry into tin, ease into base and side, trim
edge; prick base all over with fork. Place on an
oven tray. Refrigerate 20 minutes.
3 Bake pastry case 15 minutes. Cool. Spoon beef
mixture into pastry case.
4 Boil or steam potato about 20 minutes or
until soft. Add butter and milk; mash until smooth,
season to taste. Spoon mash over beef mixture;
sprinkle with cheese.
5 Bake, uncovered, about 20 minutes or until
browned. Stand pie 5 minutes before serving.

prep + cook time 1 hour 15 minutes
(+ cooling & refrigeration) **serves** 6
nutritional count per serving 35.8g total fat
(16.9g saturated fat); 2533kJ (606 cal);
43.8g carbohydrate; 26.2g protein; 3.4g fibre

tip You can use one quantity basic shortcrust pastry
(page 4) instead of the store-bought pastry sheets.

mexican beef and bean pie

¼ cup (60ml) olive oil
750g (1½ pounds) beef chuck steak,
   chopped coarsely
¼ cup (35g) plain (all-purpose) flour
1 medium brown onion (150g), chopped finely
35g (1 ounce) taco seasoning mix
2 cups (520g) bottled tomato pasta sauce
½ cup (125ml) chicken stock
400g (12½ ounces) canned red kidney beans,
   rinsed, drained
1 cup (30g) corn chips

POLENTA PASTRY
1¼ cups (185g) plain (all-purpose) flour
⅓ cup (55g) polenta
80g (2½ ounces) butter, chopped coarsely
1 egg
2 tablespoons iced water, approximately

1 Preheat oven to 180°C/350°F. Oil 24cm (9½-inch) round loose-based flan tin.
2 Heat half the oil in large saucepan; toss beef in flour, shake away excess. Cook beef, in batches, until browned. Transfer to 3-litre (12-cup) ovenproof dish. Heat remaining oil in same pan; cook onion, stirring, until softened. Add seasoning mix, cook, stirring, 1 minute. Gradually stir in sauce and stock; bring to the boil. Pour over beef. Bake, covered, 2 hours.
3 Stir beans into beef mixture; cook, uncovered, 10 minutes. Season to taste; cool.
4 Meanwhile, make pastry.
5 Roll pastry between sheets of baking paper until large enough to line tin. Lift pastry into tin, press into side; trim edge. Place on oven tray, bake about 20 minutes or until browned lightly; cool.
6 Spoon filling into pastry case. Bake about 20 minutes or until heated through. Stand pie 5 minutes; serve topped with corn chips.

POLENTA PASTRY Process flour, polenta and butter until mixture is crumbly. Add egg and most of the water; process until ingredients just come together. Knead pastry on floured surface until smooth, enclose with plastic wrap; refrigerate pastry 30 minutes.

prep + cook time 2 hours 50 minutes
(+ cooling & refrigeration) serves 6
nutritional count per serving 34.1g total fat
(12.6g saturated fat); 2717kJ (650 cal);
50.1g carbohydrate; 39g protein; 7.3g fibre

serving suggestion Serve with guacamole and sour cream.

pork sausage and apple pie

1 tablespoon olive oil
1 medium brown onion (150g), chopped finely
1 baby fennel bulb (130g), sliced thinly
6 thick pork and herb sausages (720g)
2 teaspoons plain (all-purpose) flour
1 cup (250ml) chicken stock
2 teaspoons mild english mustard
1 medium apple (150g), grated coarsely
2 tablespoons coarsely chopped fresh
 flat-leaf parsley
1 egg, beaten lightly

SHORTCRUST PASTRY
1½ cups (225g) plain (all-purpose) flour
80g (2½ ounces) cold butter, chopped coarsely
1 egg yolk
2 tablespoons iced water, approximately

1 Make shortcrust pastry.
2 Preheat oven to 200°C/400°F. Oil 1.5-litre (6-cup) ovenproof dish.
3 Heat oil in large frying pan; stir onion, fennel and mince squeezed from sausages until browned. Add flour; cook, stirring, until mixture bubbles and thickens. Gradually stir in stock and mustard, stir over heat until mixture boils and thickens, simmer, 5 minutes. Stir in apple and parsley; season. Spoon mixture into dish.
4 Roll pastry between sheets of baking paper until large enough to cover dish. Top dish with pastry, brush with egg. Bake about 30 minutes or until pastry is browned.

SHORTCRUST PASTRY Process flour and butter until crumbly. Add egg yolk and most of the water; process until ingredients just come together. Knead pastry on floured surface until smooth, enclose with plastic wrap; refrigerate 30 minutes.

prep + cook time 1 hour (+ refrigeration) **serves** 4
nutritional count per serving 64.7g total fat (28.7g saturated fat); 3892kJ (931 cal); 53.8g carbohydrate; 32g protein; 6.2g fibre

beef and caramelised onion pies

2 medium red onions (340g)
2 tablespoons olive oil
2 tablespoons brown sugar
1 cup (250ml) beer
2 cloves garlic, crushed
200g (6½ ounces) button mushrooms, sliced thinly
3 sprigs fresh thyme
500g (1 pound) minced (ground) beef
¼ cup (70g) tomato paste
2 teaspoons fresh thyme leaves
1 sheet puff pastry, quartered
1 egg, beaten lightly
1 teaspoon brown sugar, extra

1 Preheat oven to 220°C/425°F.
2 Slice onions thinly, reserving four intact small slices. Heat half the oil in large frying pan; cook onion, stirring, until soft. Add sugar and ¼ cup (60ml) of the beer; cook, stirring occasionally, about 10 minutes until onion caramelises.
3 Meanwhile, heat remaining oil in large saucepan; cook garlic, mushrooms and thyme sprigs until soft. Add beef, cook, stirring, until browned. Add paste and remaining beer. Simmer, uncovered, about 10 minutes or until thickened slightly. Stir in caramelised onion and thyme leaves; season. Discard thyme sprigs.
4 Spoon mixture into four 1-cup (250ml) ovenproof dishes. Top each with pastry; brush with egg. Sprinkle reserved onion slices with extra sugar, press gently into centre of pastry. Place dishes on oven tray. Bake about 20 minutes or until pastry is puffed and browned.

prep + cook time 1 hour **makes** 4
nutritional count per serving 28.8g total fat
(6g saturated fat); 2245kJ (537 cal);
30.3g carbohydrate; 33.3g protein; 3.9g fibre

individual beef wellingtons

2 teaspoons olive oil
750g (1½-pound) piece beef eye fillet
200g (6½ ounces) button mushrooms
2 shallots (50g), chopped coarsely
1 clove garlic, crushed
20g (¾ ounce) butter
1 tablespoon finely chopped fresh tarragon
1 tablespoon finely chopped fresh flat-leaf parsley
⅓ cup (75g) pâté
12 thin slices (180g) prosciutto
4 sheets puff pastry
1 egg, beaten lightly

1 Heat oil in large frying pan; season beef, cook over high heat until well browned all over. Remove from pan. Wrap tightly in plastic wrap to hold shape. Place on a plate; refrigerate 1 hour.
2 Meanwhile, process mushrooms, shallot and garlic until chopped finely. Heat butter in same pan; add mushroom mixture. Cook, stirring, until liquid has evaporated. Transfer to small bowl; season to taste, cool. Stir in tarragon and parsley.
3 Preheat oven to 220°C/425°F. Line oven tray with baking paper; place wire rack over tray.
4 Cut beef into four, spread top of each with pâté Put one slice prosciutto onto bench; overlap slightly with another slice and top with another slice in the centre. Spread a quarter of the mushroom mixture evenly over centre of prosciutto. Place beef, pâté-side up, on one short end of prosciutto. Enclose with prosciutto. Repeat with remaining prosciutto, mushroom mixture and beef.
5 Place beef in centre of each pastry sheet, fold two sides over to enclose beef, press pastry onto sides of beef. Trim excess pastry away. Press edges of pastry together with a fork. Cut a small steam hole on top of each wellington. Decorate with pastry scraps.
6 Place wellingtons on wire rack; brush with egg. Bake about 20 minutes for medium beef. Stand wellingtons on rack for 10 minutes before serving.

prep + cook time 1 hour 20 minutes (+ refrigeration)
makes 4
nutritional count per serving 58.8g total fat
(10.8g saturated fat); 4372kJ (1046 cal);
61.5g carbohydrate; 66g protein; 4g fibre

caramelised onion, fig and prosciutto tarts

40g (1½ ounces) butter
2 large brown onions (400g), sliced thinly
1 tablespoon brown sugar
2 sheets puff pastry
3 fresh figs (180g), quartered
80g (2½ ounces) firm blue cheese, crumbled
4 thin slices prosciutto (60g), halved
1 tablespoon balsamic glaze
20g (¾ ounce) baby rocket (arugula) leaves

1 Preheat oven to 220°C/425°F. Oil and line oven tray.
2 Heat butter in medium pan; add onion, cook covered, over low heat, about 15 minutes, stirring occasionally, until onion is soft. Stir in sugar.

3 Meanwhile, quarter pastry sheets, place on oven tray. Fold in 1cm (½-inch) borders; prick centres, bake pastry about 15 minutes or until browned.
4 Spread onion mixture into pastry cases, top with figs and cheese; bake about 3 minutes or until cheese is softened.
5 Top tarts with prosciutto, drizzle with balsamic glaze; sprinkle with rocket.

prep + cook time 35 minutes **serves** 8 as an entree
nutritional count per serving 17.4g total fat (5.6g saturated fat); 1133kJ (271 cal); 21.2g carbohydrate; 6.8g protein; 1.8g fibre

tip Fetta or goat's cheese can be used in place of the blue cheese.

spiced chorizo and bean pies

2 teaspoons olive oil

3 cured chorizo sausages (375g), halved, sliced thinly

1 medium red onion (170g), chopped finely

2 cloves garlic, crushed

¼ teaspoon dried chilli flakes

1 teaspoon each smoked paprika and ground cumin

410g (13 ounces) canned crushed tomatoes

⅓ cup (80ml) water

400g (12½ ounces) canned white beans, rinsed, drained

4 sheets fillo pastry

30g (1 ounce) butter, melted

1 Preheat oven to 220°C/425°F. Oil four 1¼-cup (310ml) ovenproof dishes.

2 Heat oil in large saucepan; cook chorizo until crisp. Remove from pan, reserving oil. Cook onion and garlic in same pan, stirring, until softened. Add spices; cook, stirring, until fragrant. Add undrained tomatoes, the water and beans. Simmer, uncovered, 5 minutes; season.

3 Spoon mixture into dishes.

4 Brush pastry sheets with butter. Scrunch and place over filling.

5 Bake pies about 15 minutes or until pastry is browned and crisp.

prep + cook time 45 minutes makes 4
nutritional count per serving 35.2g total fat (14.1g saturated fat); 1868kJ (447 cal); 16.1g carbohydrate; 15.6g protein; 4.1g fibre

55

chorizo and potato galette with green olives

2 sheets puff pastry
2 tablespoons olive oil
2 cloves garlic, chopped finely
½ teaspoon sweet paprika
2 teaspoons coarsely chopped fresh rosemary
2 small unpeeled potatoes (140g)
125g (4 ounces) cured chorizo sausage,
   sliced thinly
¼ small red onion (25g), sliced thinly
⅓ cup (90g) roasted capsicum (bell pepper) strips
¾ cup (90g) drained marinated green olives
¼ cup fresh flat-leaf parsley leaves

1 Preheat oven to 220°C/425°F. Line two oven trays with baking paper.
2 Place pastry on trays. Combine oil, garlic, paprika and rosemary in small bowl. Brush half the oil mixture over pastry, leaving a 1cm (½-inch) border.
3 Slice potatoes thinly using mandolin or V-slicer. Top pastry pieces with single layer of potato; brush with remaining oil mixture; season.
4 Bake 10 minutes. Top with chorizo, onion and capsicum; bake about 10 minutes or until pastry is crisp.
5 Top galettes with olives and parsley.

prep + cook time 30 minutes serves 4
nutritional count per serving 36.8g total fat
(5.8g saturated fat); 2257kJ (540 cal);
41.5g carbohydrate; 9.9g protein; 3g fibre

lamb and rosemary pies with scone topping

2 teaspoons olive oil
5 thick lamb and rosemary sausages (750g)
1 medium brown onion (150g), chopped finely
1 tablespoon plain (all-purpose) flour
1¼ cups (310ml) chicken stock
1 tablespoon honey
2 tablespoons coarsely chopped fresh rosemary
1 tablespoon milk
4 sprigs fresh rosemary

SCONE TOPPING
1 cup (150g) self-raising flour
60g (2 ounces) butter, chopped coarsely
¼ cup (20g) finely grated parmesan cheese
½ cup (125ml) milk, approximately

1 Preheat oven to 200°C/400°F. Oil four 1¼-cup (310ml) ovenproof dishes.
2 Heat oil in large frying pan. Cook sausages until browned and cooked through; slice thinly. Cook onion in same pan, stirring, until tender. Add flour; cook, stirring, until mixture bubbles and thickens. Stir in stock, honey and chopped rosemary, stir over heat until mixture boils and thickens; simmer 3 minutes. Return sausage to pan. Season.
3 Meanwhile, make scone topping.
4 Spoon hot filling into dishes. Top with scone topping. Brush with milk; press a rosemary sprig into top of each pie. Bake about 25 minutes or until browned.

SCONE TOPPING Place flour in medium bowl; rub in butter, stir in parmesan. Stir in enough milk to make a soft sticky dough. Divide dough into four, knead into rounds to fit dishes.

prep + cook time 55 minutes **makes** 4
nutritional count per serving 36.8g total fat (19.2g saturated fat); 2822kJ (675 cal); 38.7g carbohydrate; 46.9g protein; 2g fibre

lamb shank pies with crushed peas and fetta

6 french-trimmed lamb shanks (1.5kg)
¼ cup (35g) plain (all-purpose) flour
1 tablespoon olive oil
2 medium brown onions (300g), chopped coarsely
2 medium carrots (240g), chopped coarsely
3 cloves garlic, crushed
½ teaspoon dried oregano
3 cups (750ml) salt-reduced chicken stock
1 cup (260g) bottled tomato pasta sauce
2 medium potatoes (400g), chopped coarsely
2 tablespoons lemon juice
2 tablespoons chopped fresh dill
2 sheets butter puff pastry
1 egg, beaten lightly

CRUSHED PEAS AND FETTA
2½ cups (300g) frozen baby peas
1 tablespoon torn fresh mint leaves
1 tablespoon olive oil
⅓ cup (65g) crumbled fetta cheese

1 Preheat oven to 180°C/350°F.
2 Toss shanks in flour; shake away excess. Heat oil in medium flameproof dish; cook shanks until browned. Remove from dish.
3 Add onion and carrot to same dish; cook, stirring, until soft. Add garlic and oregano; cook, stirring, until fragrant. Add stock and sauce; bring to the boil. Return shanks to dish; cover tightly. Transfer to oven; cook for 1½ hours.

4 Add potato to dish; cover, cook 30 minutes or until lamb and potato are tender. If sauce is too thin, simmer, uncovered, over medium heat until thickened slightly. Stir in juice and dill; season to taste. Cool 10 minutes.
5 Remove half the meat from the shanks; cut meat into smaller pieces. Refrigerate lamb mixture and shanks 3 hours or until cold. Remove fat from surface of dish.
6 Preheat oven to 220°C/425°F.
7 Divide lamb mixture and shanks among six 2-cup (500ml) deep ovenproof dishes, standing shanks upright in dishes. Cut out pastry slightly larger than the tops of the dishes. Cut a small cross in the centre of each pastry.
8 Place pastry over pies, inserting shank bone through cross in pastry. Brush pastry with egg. Place dishes on oven tray. Bake about 20 minutes or until browned.
9 Meanwhile, make crushed peas and fetta, serve with pies.

CRUSHED PEAS AND FETTA Boil, steam or microwave peas until tender; drain. Crush peas lightly with fork. Stir in mint and oil; season to taste. Gently stir in cheese.

prep + cook time 3 hours 10 minutes (+ cooling & refrigeration) serves 6
nutritional count per serving 36g total fat (15.5g saturated fat); 2876kJ (688 cal); 45.3g carbohydrate; 42.1g protein; 7.6g fibre

serving suggestion Serve with lemon wedges.

rogan josh lamb pie with coriander chutney

1kg (2 pounds) diced lamb shoulder
⅓ cup (50g) plain (all-purpose) flour
2 tablespoons vegetable oil
2 medium brown onions (300g), sliced thinly
½ cup (135g) rogan josh curry paste
410g (13 ounces) canned diced tomatoes
2 cups (500ml) salt-reduced beef stock
1 sheet puff pastry
2 teaspoons milk
¼ teaspoon cumin seeds

CORIANDER CHUTNEY
1 tablespoon lemon juice
1 teaspoon sugar
pinch ground cumin
1 fresh long green chilli, chopped coarsely
1 cup firmly packed fresh coriander
 (cilantro) leaves
1 cup firmly packed fresh mint leaves
½ cup (140g) thick yogurt

1 Toss lamb in flour, shake away excess. Heat oil
in large saucepan; cook lamb, in batches, until well
browned. Remove from pan. Add onion to same
pan; cook, stirring, until softened.
2 Add paste to pan; cook, stirring, until fragrant.
Return lamb to pan with undrained tomatoes and
stock; bring to the boil, simmer, covered, 1½ hours.
Simmer, uncovered, about 30 minutes or until
tender. Season to taste; cool.
3 Preheat oven to 220°C/425°F.
4 Spoon curry into 24cm (9½-inch) pie dish
(1.5-litre/6-cup). Score pastry in criss-cross pattern.
Place pastry over filling; trim edge. Brush pastry
with milk, sprinkle with seeds. Place on oven tray;
bake, uncovered, about 30 minutes or until browned.
5 Meanwhile, make coriander chutney.
6 Serve pie with chutney.

CORIANDER CHUTNEY Blend all ingredients until
smooth; season to taste.

prep + cook time 3 hours (+ cooling) **serves** 6
nutritional count per serving 30.9g total fat
(8g saturated fat); 2337kJ (559 cal);
26.8g carbohydrate; 40.9g protein; 4.7g fibre

tip Ask the butcher for lamb shoulder as what is
sold as diced lamb is sometimes from the leg and
will not be as tender.

old-fashioned lamb and celeriac pie

1.25kg (2½ pounds) diced lamb shoulder
½ cup (75g) plain (all-purpose) flour
2 tablespoons olive oil
1 large brown onion (200g), chopped
1 large carrot (180g), chopped
750g (1½ pounds) celeriac (celery root), trimmed,
    chopped coarsely
1½ cups (375ml) salt-reduced beef stock
2 teaspoons chopped fresh thyme
2 tablespoons chopped fresh flat-leaf parsley
1 egg, beaten lightly

SHORTCRUST PASTRY
1½ cups (225g) plain (all-purpose) flour
125g (4 ounces) butter, chopped coarsely
1 egg yolk
2 tablespoons iced water, approximately

1   Toss lamb in flour; shake away excess. Heat oil
in large saucepan; cook lamb, in batches, until
browned. Remove from pan.
2   Add onion, carrot and celeriac to pan; cook,
stirring, 5 minutes. Return lamb to pan with stock
and herbs; simmer, covered, about 2 hours or until
tender. Season to taste; cool.
3   Meanwhile, make shortcrust pastry.
4   Preheat oven to 180°C/350°F.
5   Spoon lamb mixture into 2-litre (8-cup)
ovenproof dish; place on oven tray.
6   Roll pastry between sheets of baking paper until
large enough to cover top of dish. Brush edge of
dish with egg. Place pastry over filling, trim edge;
pinch edge in decorative pattern. Brush pastry with
egg. Bake about 35 minutes or until browned.

SHORTCRUST PASTRY Process flour and butter
until crumbly. Add egg yolk and most of the water;
process until ingredients just come together. Knead
pastry on floured surface until smooth, enclose with
plastic wrap; refrigerate 1 hour.

prep + cook time 3 hours
(+ refrigeration & cooling) **serves** 6
nutritional count per serving 37.7g total fat
(18.4g saturated fat); 3060kJ (732 cal);
43g carbohydrate; 51.9g protein; 6.5g fibre

tip Ask the butcher for lamb shoulder as what is
sold as diced lamb is sometimes from the leg and
will not be as tender.

curried beef and pea pie

1 tablespoon olive oil
1 large brown onion (200g), chopped finely
4 cloves garlic, crushed
600g minced (ground) beef
2 tablespoons curry powder
2 tablespoons plain (all-purpose) flour
2 tablespoons tomato paste
2 cups (500ml) beef stock
¾ cup (90g) frozen peas
1 sheet puff pastry
1 egg, beaten lightly

1 Preheat oven to 220°C/425°F. Oil 1.5-litre (6-cup) ovenproof dish.
2 Heat oil in large saucepan; cook onion and garlic, stirring, until onion softens. Add beef; cook, stirring, until browned.

3 Add curry powder, cook, stirring, until fragrant. Add flour; cook, stirring, until mixture bubbles and thickens. Add paste; gradually stir in stock; stir until mixture boils and thickens; simmer, uncovered, 10 minutes. Stir in peas; season to taste.
4 Pour mixture into dish. Top with pastry; trim edge. Brush with egg; sprinkle with a little extra curry powder.
5 Bake about 20 minutes or until pastry is puffed and browned lightly.

prep + cook time 45 minutes **serves** 4
nutritional count per serving 27.2g total fat (7.4g saturated fat); 2128kJ (509 cal); 26.1g carbohydrate; 38.5g protein; 3.6g fibre

sausage, egg and bacon pies

3 rindless bacon slices (240g), halved
2 thick sausages (300g)
3 sheets shortcrust pastry
1 cup (260g) bottled tomato pasta sauce
6 eggs
2 green onions (scallions), sliced thinly

1 Preheat oven to 220°C/425°F. Oil six-hole
(¾ cup/180ml) texas muffin pan.
2 Cook bacon in large frying pan until browned
and crisp; drain on absorbent paper. Cook
sausages in same pan until browned all over and
cooked through; cool. Slice sausages thinly.

3 Cut two 13cm (5½-inch) rounds from each pastry
sheet; press rounds into pan holes. Prick bases with
fork. Line bases and sides of each pan hole with
bacon. Top with sausage; pour over sauce. Bake
10 minutes.
4 Using a spoon, make an indent in sauce.
Crack an egg carefully into each pie; bake about
15 minutes or until egg is set.
5 Serve sprinkled with onion.

prep + cook time 50 minutes (+ cooling) **makes** 6
nutritional count per serving 45g total fat
(21.1g saturated fat); 2847kJ (681 cal);
41.6g carbohydrate; 26.7g protein; 3.8g fibre

moroccan-style lamb pies with harissa yogurt

1.25kg (2½ pounds) diced lamb shoulder
½ cup (75g) plain (all-purpose) flour
2 tablespoons olive oil
2 medium brown onions (300g), chopped finely
2 medium carrots (240g), chopped finely
2 cloves garlic, crushed
1 teaspoon each ground coriander, cumin, ginger
  and turmeric
1 cinnamon stick
1½ cups (375ml) beef stock
6 fresh dates (150g), seeded, chopped coarsely
1 tablespoon honey
2 tablespoons finely chopped fresh
  coriander (cilantro)
8 sheets fillo pastry
50g (1½ ounces) butter, melted
2 teaspoons sesame seeds

HARISSA YOGURT
¾ cup (200g) thick yogurt
2 tablespoons harissa

1 Toss lamb in flour; shake away excess. Heat oil in large saucepan; cook lamb, in batches, until browned. Remove from pan.
2 Add onion and carrot to pan; cook, stirring, until soft. Add garlic and spices; cook, stirring, until fragrant. Return lamb to pan with stock; simmer, covered, 1½ hours.
3 Preheat oven to 220°C/425°F.
4 Simmer lamb, uncovered, about 30 minutes or until tender and sauce is thickened. Stir in dates, honey and coriander; season to taste.
5 Spoon mixture into eight 1-cup (250ml) ovenproof dishes. Brush each pastry sheet with butter, scrunch and place over filling. Sprinkle with seeds. Bake, uncovered, about 15 minutes or until browned.
6 Meanwhile, make harissa yogurt.
7 Serve pies with harissa yogurt.

HARISSA YOGURT Combine yogurt and half the harissa in small bowl. Serve topped with remaining harissa.

prep + cook time 3 hours 15 minutes (+ cooling)
serves 8
nutritional count per serving 22.2g total fat
(10g saturated fat); 1981kJ (474 cal);
30.1g carbohydrate; 36.9g protein; 3.2g fibre

tip Ask the butcher for lamb shoulder as what is sold as diced lamb is sometimes from the leg and will not be as tender.
note Harissa is a Tunisian hot chilli paste, available in delicatessens and gourmet food stores. As every brand is different, add it gradually, a teaspoon at a time, until the desired heat is reached. We used a mild harissa.

mushroom and pancetta quiche

60g (2 ounces) butter
3 shallots (75g), chopped finely
200g (6½ ounces) button mushrooms,
  sliced thickly
100g (3 ounces) swiss brown mushrooms,
  sliced thickly
2 cloves garlic, crushed
¾ cup (180g) sour cream
2 eggs
100g (3 ounces) thinly sliced pancetta

SHORTCRUST PASTRY
1½ cups (225g) plain (all-purpose) flour
125g (4 ounces) butter, chopped coarsely
1 egg yolk
2 tablespoons iced water, approximately

1 Make shortcrust pastry.
2 Roll pastry between sheets of baking paper until
large enough to line 28cm (11-inch) loose-based
flan tin. Lift pastry into tin; press into side, leaving
edge overhanging slightly. Place tin on oven tray;
refrigerate 30 minutes.
3 Meanwhile, preheat oven to 180°C/350°F.
4 Cover pastry with baking paper, fill with dried
beans or rice. Bake 15 minutes. Remove paper and
beans; bake 15 minutes. Trim pastry edge with a
sharp knife.
5 Heat butter in large frying pan. Add shallot;
cook, stirring, until softened. Add mushrooms;
cook, stirring, until softened. Stir in garlic; cook,
stirring, until fragrant. Season to taste; cool.
6 Spoon mushroom mixture into pastry case.
Combine sour cream and eggs in medium bowl;
season. Pour egg mixture over mushrooms. Top
with pancetta. Bake about 25 minutes or until set.

SHORTCRUST PASTRY Process flour and butter
until crumbly. Add egg yolk and most of the water;
process until ingredients just come together. Knead
pastry on floured surface until smooth, enclose in
plastic wrap; refrigerate 1 hour.

prep + cook time 1 hour 40 minutes
(+ refrigeration) serves 8
nutritional count per serving 32.8g total fat
(19.9g saturated fat); 1772kJ (424 cal);
22.1g carbohydrate; 10g protein; 2.2g fibre

penang pork curry pies

1 tablespoon peanut oil
½ cup (150g) penang curry paste
500g minced (ground) pork
2 kaffir lime leaves, torn
1⅔ cups (400ml) coconut milk
⅓ cup (80ml) water
2 tablespoons fish sauce
¼ cup (65g) grated palm sugar
150g (5½ ounces) green beans, chopped coarsely
100g (3 ounces) broccoli, chopped finely
1 small red capsicum (bell pepper) (150g),
  chopped finely
225g (7 ounces) canned bamboo shoots, drained
¼ cup coarsely chopped fresh coriander (cilantro)
2 sheets puff pastry
1 egg, beaten lightly

1 Heat oil in large saucepan; add paste; cook,
stirring, until fragrant. Add pork; cook, stirring, until
changed in colour. Stir in lime leaves, coconut
milk, the water, sauce and sugar; bring to the boil.
Simmer, uncovered, about 10 minutes or until
reduced slightly.
2 Add beans, broccoli, capsicum and bamboo
shoots; simmer, uncovered, about 3 minutes or
until vegetables are tender. Stir in coriander.
Discard lime leaves; cool.
3 Meanwhile, preheat oven to 220°C/425°F.
4 Spoon pork mixture into four 1½-cup (375ml)
ovenproof dishes.
5 Cut pastry a little larger than the tops of the
dishes. Brush edge of dishes with egg. Place pastry
over filling; place dishes on oven tray, brush with a
little egg. Bake about 15 minutes or until pastry is
browned and puffed.

prep + cook time 1 hour (+ cooling) **serves** 4
nutritional count per serving 57.5g total fat
(24.2g saturated fat); 3741kJ (895 cal);
55.1g carbohydrate; 37.9g protein; 7.2g fibre

eggplant and hummus lamb tarts

¼ cup (60ml) olive oil
2 tablespoons lemon juice
1 clove garlic, crushed
1 tablespoon finely chopped fresh flat-leaf parsley
1 tablespoon finely chopped fresh rosemary
500g (1 pound) lamb eye of loin (backstrap)
1 small eggplant (230g), sliced thinly
1 tablespoon coarse cooking (kosher) salt
1 sheet puff pastry
1 egg, beaten lightly
1 tablespoon olive oil, extra
50g (1½ ounces) baby spinach leaves
¼ cup (40g) seeded small black olives

HUMMUS
¼ cup (60ml) hot water
1½ tablespoons lemon juice
1 tablespoon olive oil
1 tablespoon tahini
1 clove garlic, chopped finely
1 teaspoon sea salt flakes
400g (12½ ounces) canned chickpeas (garbanzos),
  rinsed, drained

1 Combine oil with juice, garlic and herbs in jug; reserve ¼ cup (60ml) marinade. Pour remaining mixture over lamb in shallow dish; turn to coat. Cover, refrigerate 2 hours.
2 Meanwhile, place eggplant in colander, sprinkle with salt. Stand eggplant 30 minutes. Rinse eggplant; pat dry.
3 Make hummus.
4 Preheat oven to 220°C/425°F.
5 Cut pastry in half. Place pastry on baking-paper-lined oven tray. Prick pastry well with fork; brush pastry lightly with egg. Bake about 15 minutes or until puffed and browned.
6 Brush eggplant with extra oil; cook on heated oiled grill pan (or grill or barbecue) until browned on both sides and tender.
7 Season lamb, cook on grill pan until browned both sides and done as desired. Remove from pan; cover, stand 5 minutes before slicing thinly.
8 Spread hummus thickly over base of tarts, top with eggplant, lamb, spinach and olives; drizzle tarts with the reserved marinade.

HUMMUS Blend ingredients until smooth; season to taste.

prep + cook time 1 hour (+ refrigeration) serves 4
nutritional count per serving 44.6g total fat
(7.1g saturated fat); 2968kJ (710 cal);
28.5g carbohydrate; 46.2g protein; 6.4g fibre

serving suggestion Serve with lemon wedges.
tip For a shortcut, use store-bought hummus and well-drained chargrilled eggplant.

vegetable pies

vegetable and lentil potato pie

½ cup (100g) french-style green lentils
1 tablespoon olive oil
1 medium brown onion (150g), chopped finely
1 medium carrot (120g), chopped coarsely
2 stalks celery (300g), trimmed, chopped coarsely
1 medium parsnip (250g), chopped coarsely
2 cloves garlic, crushed
200g (6½ ounces) button mushrooms, sliced thickly
2 bay leaves
1 tablespoon finely chopped fresh rosemary
¼ cup (70g) tomato paste
1 cup (250ml) vegetable stock
410g (13 ounces) canned diced tomatoes
150g (4½ ounces) green beans, trimmed, chopped coarsely
300g (9½ ounces) potatoes, chopped coarsely
300g (9½ ounces) kumara (orange sweet potato), chopped coarsely
60g (2 ounces) butter
½ cup (40g) finely grated parmesan cheese

1 Cook lentils in large saucepan of boiling water until tender; drain.
2 Meanwhile, heat oil in large saucepan; cook onion, carrot, celery, parsnip and garlic, stirring, until vegetables soften. Add mushrooms, bay leaves and rosemary; cook, stirring, until fragrant. Stir in paste, stock and undrained tomatoes; bring to the boil. Reduce heat; simmer, uncovered, about 20 minutes or until thickened. Add beans and lentils; cook, stirring, about 3 minutes or until beans are tender. Season to taste.
3 Meanwhile, boil, steam or microwave potato and kumara, separately, until tender; drain. Mash potato with half the butter until smooth; season to taste. Mash kumara with remaining butter until smooth; season to taste.
4 Preheat oven to 200°C/400°F.
5 Spoon lentil mixture into 2-litre (8-cup) ovenproof dish. Top with potato mash. Swirl through kumara mash; sprinkle with cheese. Bake, uncovered, about 30 minutes or until cheese is browned.

prep + cook time 1 hour 15 minutes serves 6
nutritional count per serving 14.5g total fat (7.3g saturated fat); 1296kJ (310 cal); 28.4g carbohydrate; 12.8g protein; 8.7g fibre

olive and roasted tomato tart

250g (8 ounces) cherry tomatoes, halved
¼ cup (65g) chunky basil pesto dip
4 eggs
¾ cup (180ml) pouring cream
1 small red onion (100g), sliced thinly
⅓ cup (55g) seeded black olives, halved
⅓ cup (80g) ricotta cheese, crumbled
20g (¾ ounce) baby rocket (arugula) leaves

SHORTCRUST PASTRY
1½ cups (225g) plain (all-purpose) flour
125g (4 ounces) cold butter, chopped coarsely
1 egg yolk
1 tablespoon iced water, approximately

1 Make shortcrust pastry.
2 Preheat oven to 180°C/350°F. Line oven tray with baking paper.
3 Place tomatoes, cut-side up, on tray. Bake about 20 minutes or until tender.
4 Oil 24cm (9½-inch) round loose-based flan tin. Roll pastry between sheets of baking paper until large enough to line tin. Lift pastry into tin; press into side, trim edge, prick base all over with fork. Refrigerate 20 minutes.
5 Increase oven to 200°C/400°F. Place tin on oven tray; cover pastry with baking paper, fill with dried beans or rice. Bake 10 minutes. Remove paper and beans; bake 5 minutes; cool.
6 Reduce oven to 180°C/350°F.
7 Spread pastry with dip. Whisk eggs and cream in large jug; season. Place tomatoes over dip, pour over egg mixture. Top with onion, olives and cheese. Bake about 45 minutes or until set. Top with rocket.

SHORTCRUST PASTRY Process flour and butter until crumbly. Add egg yolk and most of the water; process until ingredients just come together. Enclose in plastic wrap; refrigerate 30 minutes.

prep + cook time 1 hour 40 minutes
(+ refrigeration) serves 6
nutritional count per serving 40.9g total fat
(23.2g saturated fat); 2295kJ (549 cal);
32.3g carbohydrate; 12.7g protein; 2.7g fibre

double-crust pizza

1 medium brown onion (150g), sliced thinly
1 large zucchini (150g), sliced thinly
1 medium red capsicum (bell pepper) (200g),
  sliced thinly
2 cloves garlic, crushed
½ cup (75g) sun-dried tomato strips
½ cup (75g) seeded black olives, halved
280g (9 ounces) artichokes in brine, drained, halved
½ cup (140g) tomato paste
1 cup (100g) coarsely grated mozzarella cheese
1 egg, beaten lightly

PIZZA DOUGH
2 cups (300g) plain (all-purpose) flour
1½ teaspoons (7g) dry yeast
½ teaspoon salt
¾ cup (180ml) water
2 tablespoons olive oil

1 Make pizza dough.
2 Meanwhile, heat remaining oil in large frying pan; cook onion, zucchini, capsicum and garlic, stirring, until vegetables are tender. Remove from heat; add tomato, olives and artichokes.
3 Preheat oven to 200°C/400°F. Oil oven tray.
4 Turn dough onto floured surface; divide in half. Roll one portion to a 30cm (12-inch) round. Transfer to tray. Spread paste over base, top with filling, leaving a 2cm (¾-inch) border. Sprinkle with cheese; brush edge with a little egg. Roll remaining dough to a 30cm (12-inch) round. Cover filling with dough, press edges to seal. Brush with egg.
5 Cut three slashes in centre of pie. Bake about 30 minutes or until browned. Stand 5 minutes.

PIZZA DOUGH Place flour, yeast and salt in large bowl; gradually stir in the water and half the oil, mix to a soft dough. Knead dough on floured surface about 5 minutes or until elastic; place in large oiled bowl, turn once to coat in oil. Cover; stand in a warm place about 1 hour or until dough doubles.

prep + cook time 1 hour (+ standing) serves 6
nutritional count per serving 12.3g total fat
(3.7g saturated fat); 1609kJ (385 cal);
49.1g carbohydrate; 15.3g protein; 7g fibre

roasted garlicky pumpkin and sage pies

900g (1¾ pounds) butternut pumpkin,
  chopped coarsely
4 cloves garlic, unpeeled
1 tablespoon olive oil
3 eggs, beaten lightly
½ cup (125ml) pouring cream
¼ cup coarsely chopped fresh sage
75g (2½ ounces) fetta cheese
1½ tablespoons pine nuts

SPICY PASTRY
1½ cups (225g) plain (all-purpose) flour
1 teaspoon ground coriander
1 teaspoon cumin seeds
125g (4 ounces) cold butter, chopped coarsely
1 egg yolk
2 tablespoons iced water, approximately

1 Preheat oven to 220°C/425°F.
2 Place pumpkin and garlic on baking-paper-lined oven tray, drizzle with oil. Bake about 20 minutes or until tender. Transfer to large bowl; cool 5 minutes. Squeeze garlic from skins. Mash pumpkin and garlic coarsely with a fork. Stir in eggs, cream and sage; season.
3 Meanwhile, make spicy pastry.
4 Grease six 9cm x 12cm (3½-inch x 5-inch) oval pie tins. Divide pastry into six even pieces. Roll each piece between sheets of baking paper until large enough to line tins. Lift pastry into tins; press into side, trim edge. Refrigerate 20 minutes.
5 Reduce oven to 200°C/400°F. Place tins on oven tray; cover pastry with baking paper, fill with dried beans or rice. Bake 10 minutes. Remove paper and beans; bake about 5 minutes or until browned lightly. Cool.
6 Fill pastry cases with pumpkin mixture. Sprinkle with crumbled cheese and nuts. Bake about 35 minutes or until set and browned.

SPICY PASTRY Process flour, spices and butter until crumbly. Add egg yolk and most of the water; process until ingredients just come together. Enclose pastry in plastic wrap; refrigerate 30 minutes.

prep + cook time 1 hour 30 minutes
(+ refrigeration) makes 6
nutritional count per serving 40g total fat
(21.3g saturated fat); 2353kJ (563 cal);
36.2g carbohydrate; 14g protein; 3.5g fibre

four-bean chilli pie with cornbread crust

1 tablespoon olive oil
1 medium brown onion (150g), chopped finely
1 medium green capsicum (bell pepper)
  (200g), chopped finely
2 cloves garlic, crushed
2 teaspoons mexican chilli powder
1 teaspoon ground cumin
800g (1½ pounds) canned diced tomatoes
1½ cups (375ml) vegetable stock
400g (12½ ounces) canned borlotti beans,
  rinsed, drained
400g (12½ ounces) canned black beans,
  rinsed, drained
400g (12½ ounces) canned red kidney beans,
  rinsed, drained
400g (12½ ounces) canned cannellini beans,
  rinsed, drained
¼ cup finely chopped fresh coriander (cilantro)
¾ cup (110g) self-raising flour
¾ cup (125g) polenta
90g (3 ounces) butter, chopped coarsely
1 egg, beaten lightly
⅓ cup (40g) coarsely grated cheddar cheese
125g (4 ounces) canned corn kernels, drained
2 tablespoons milk, approximately

1 Heat oil in large saucepan; cook onion,
capsicum and garlic, stirring, until onion softens.
Add chilli and cumin; cook, stirring, until fragrant.
Add undrained tomatoes, stock and beans; bring
to the boil. Reduce heat; simmer, uncovered, about
15 minutes or until sauce has thickened slightly. Stir
in coriander; season to taste.
2 Meanwhile, preheat oven to 200°C/400°F. Place
flour and polenta in medium bowl; rub in butter.
Stir in egg, cheese, corn and enough milk to make
a soft, sticky dough.
3 Spoon bean mixture into 2-litre (8-cup)
ovenproof dish. Drop level tablespoons of corn
mixture on top of bean mixture. Bake, uncovered,
about 20 minutes or until browned.

prep + cook time 1 hour **serves** 6
nutritional count per serving 21.2g total fat
(10.8g saturated fat); 2345kJ (561 cal);
62.9g carbohydrate; 21.4g protein; 15.7g fibre

quiche primavera

170g (5½ ounces) asparagus, trimmed, halved
60g (2 ounces) green beans, trimmed,
 halved lengthways
¼ cup (30g) frozen peas
4 eggs
½ cup (125ml) pouring cream
½ cup (120g) sour cream
1 small zucchini (90g), sliced into ribbons
1 green onion (scallion), sliced thinly
¼ cup small fresh mint leaves

SHORTCRUST PASTRY
1½ cups (225g) plain (all-purpose) flour
125g (4 ounces) cold butter, chopped coarsely
1 egg yolk
2 tablespoons iced water, approximately

1 Make shortcrust pastry.
2 Oil 24cm (9½-inch) round loose-based flan tin.
Roll pastry between sheets of baking paper until
large enough to line tin. Lift pastry into tin; press
into side, trim edge. Refrigerate 20 minutes.
3 Preheat oven to 200°C/400°F.
4 Place tin on oven tray; cover pastry with baking
paper, fill with dried beans or rice. Bake 10 minutes.
Remove paper and beans; bake 5 minutes or until
browned lightly. Cool. Reduce oven to 180°C/350°F.
5 Meanwhile, boil, steam or microwave asparagus,
beans and peas, separately, until just tender; drain.
Refresh under cold water.
6 Whisk eggs, cream and sour cream together in
large jug; season. Arrange asparagus, beans, peas
and zucchini in pastry case; sprinkle with onion.
Pour over egg mixture. Bake about 45 minutes or
until just set. Sprinkle with mint leaves.

SHORTCRUST PASTRY Blend or process flour and
butter until crumbly. Add egg yolk and most of the
water; process until ingredients just come together.
Enclose in plastic wrap; refrigerate 30 minutes.

prep + cook time 1 hour 45 minutes
(+ refrigeration) serves 6
nutritional count per serving 30.1g total fat
(23.9g saturated fat); 2165kJ (518 cal);
30g carbohydrate; 11.5g protein; 2.8g fibre

spiced green pea and potato pasties

1 tablespoon olive oil
2 medium brown onions (300g), sliced thinly
1 tablespoon caster (superfine) sugar
1 tablespoon moroccan seasoning
2 cloves garlic, crushed
1 teaspoon fresh thyme leaves
1 medium potato (200g), chopped coarsely
350g (11 ounces) butternut pumpkin,
  chopped coarsely
⅔ cup (80g) frozen peas
5 sheets shortcrust pastry
1 egg, beaten lightly
2 teaspoons sesame seeds

1 Heat oil in large frying pan; cook onion and sugar, stirring, about 15 minutes or until caramelised. Stir in seasoning, garlic and thyme. Cook, stirring, until fragrant; transfer to large bowl.
2 Meanwhile, boil, steam or microwave potato and pumpkin, separately, until tender; drain. Add potato, pumpkin and peas to bowl. Stir gently to combine; season to taste, cool.
3 Preheat oven to 200°C/400°F. Line oven trays with baking paper.
4 Cut 10 x 13cm (5¼-inch) rounds from pastry. Spoon ⅓ cup potato mixture on each round; brush edges with egg. Bring pastry edges together to form a semi-circle. Pinch edges together to seal.
5 Place pasties on trays. Brush with egg; sprinkle with seeds. Bake about 30 minutes or until browned lightly.

prep + cook time 1 hour (+ cooling) **makes** 10
nutritional count per serving 25.7g total fat (12.6g saturated fat); 1868kJ (447 cal); 45g carbohydrate; 8g protein; 3.1g fibre

sun-dried tomato and asparagus tart

250g (8 ounces) asparagus, trimmed, halved
2 sheets shortcrust pastry
3 eggs
⅓ cup (80ml) pouring cream
⅓ cup (25g) finely grated pecorino cheese
½ cup (75g) sun-dried tomatoes in oil,
  drained, sliced thinly
60g (2 ounces) fetta cheese, crumbled
1 teaspoon fresh thyme leaves

1 Boil, steam or microwave asparagus until tender; drain. Refresh under cold water; drain.
2 Line base and sides of 11.5cm x 34cm (4½-inch x 13½-inch) rectangular loose-based flan tin with pastry, joining pastry where needed. Trim excess. Place tin in freezer 20 minutes.

3 Preheat oven to 200°C/400°F.
4 Place tin on oven tray. Line pastry case with baking paper. Fill with dried beans or rice. Bake 10 minutes. Remove beans and paper. Bake about 5 minutes or until browned lightly; cool 5 minutes. Reduce oven to 180°C/350°F.
5 Whisk eggs, cream and pecorino together in large jug; season. Place asparagus into pastry case. Pour over egg mixture. Top with tomato, fetta and thyme. Bake about 25 minutes or until set.

prep + cook time 1 hour 5 minutes (+ freezing)
serves 4
nutritional count per serving 41.6g total fat (22.5g saturated fat); 2658kJ (636 cal); 45.1g carbohydrate; 18.8g protein; 5.2g fibre

tip You can use one quantity of shortcrust pastry, page 4, instead of the store-bought sheets.

mini vegetable curry pies

1 tablespoon vegetable oil
2 green onions (scallions), sliced thinly
1 medium red capsicum (bell pepper) (200g),
  chopped finely
1 medium potato (200g), chopped finely
1 medium zucchini (120g), chopped finely
1 medium carrot (120g), chopped finely
⅓ cup (100g) mild curry paste
2 cups (500ml) vegetable stock
125g (4 ounces) canned corn kernels, drained
½ cup (80g) frozen peas
3 sheets shortcrust pastry
2 sheets puff pastry
1 egg, beaten lightly
1 teaspoon cracked black pepper

1 Heat oil in large frying pan; cook onion,
capsicum, potato, zucchini and carrot, stirring, until
softened. Stir in paste, cook until fragrant. Add
stock; bring to the boil. Reduce heat to medium,
simmer, uncovered, until potato is tender and stock
evaporated. Stir in corn and peas, remove from
heat; season to taste. Cool.
2 Preheat oven to 200°C/400°F. Oil a 12-hole
(⅓-cup/80ml) muffin pan. Cut 12 x 9cm (3½-inch)
rounds from shortcrust pastry. Line pan holes with
pastry. Fill with vegetable mixture. Cut 12 x 7.5cm
(3-inch) rounds from puff pastry. Brush one side of
rounds with egg. Place rounds, egg side down over
filling; press edges to seal. Brush tops with egg.
Sprinkle with pepper.
3 Bake pies about 30 minutes or until browned.
Stand 5 minutes before serving.

prep + cook time 1 hour 10 minutes **makes** 12
nutritional count per serving 22.3g total fat
(7.1g saturated fat); 1555kJ (372 cal);
34.6g carbohydrate; 7g protein; 3.2g fibre

onion and smoked cheddar tarts

1 tablespoon olive oil
2 large brown onions (400g), sliced thinly
4 eggs
¾ cup (180ml) pouring cream
⅔ cup (80g) finely grated smoked cheddar cheese
1½ teaspoons fresh thyme leaves

PARMESAN PASTRY
1½ cups (225g) plain (all-purpose) flour
⅓ cup (25g) finely grated parmesan cheese
100g (3 ounces) cold butter, chopped coarsely
1 egg yolk
2 tablespoons iced water, approximately

1 Make parmesan pastry.
2 Oil six 9cm (3½-inch) round, loose-based flan tins. Divide pastry into six even pieces. Roll each piece of pastry between sheets of baking paper until large enough to line tins. Lift pastry into tins; press into side, trim edge. Cover; refrigerate 20 minutes.
3 Preheat oven to 200°C/400°F.
4 Place tins on oven tray; cover pastry with baking paper, fill with dried beans or rice. Bake 10 minutes. Remove paper and beans; bake about 5 minutes or until browned lightly, cool.
5 Meanwhile, heat oil in large frying pan; cook onion, stirring, about 15 minutes or until caramelised. Remove from heat.
6 Whisk eggs and cream together in large jug; season. Place onion in pastry cases. Pour over egg mixture; sprinkle with cheese and thyme. Bake about 25 minutes or until set.

PARMESAN PASTRY Blend or process flour, cheese and butter until crumbly. Add egg yolk and most of the water; process until ingredients just come together. Enclose pastry in plastic wrap; refrigerate 30 minutes.

prep + cook time 1 hour 20 minutes
(+ refrigeration) makes 6
nutritional count per serving 40.5g total fat
(23.2g saturated fat); 2312kJ (553 cal);
31.7g carbohydrate; 15.6g protein; 2.3g fibre

sweet pies & tarts

citrus-trio meringue pie

185g (6 ounces) plain sweet biscuits
90g (3 ounces) unsalted butter, melted
½ cup (75g) cornflour (cornstarch)
1¼ cups (275g) caster (superfine) sugar
¼ cup (60ml) each orange, lemon and lime juice
1 cup (250ml) water
80g (2½ ounces) unsalted butter, extra
3 eggs, separated
2 teaspoons each finely grated orange, lemon
   and lime rind

1 Grease 24cm (9½-inch) round, 2cm-deep loose-based flan tin.
2 Blend or process biscuits until fine. Transfer to medium bowl; stir in melted butter.
3 Press biscuit mixture evenly over base and side of tin, place on oven tray; refrigerate 30 minutes.
4 Combine cornflour and ½ cup (110g) of the sugar in medium saucepan; gradually stir in juices and the water until smooth. Stir over high heat until mixture boils and thickens. Reduce heat; simmer, stirring, 1 minute. Remove from heat; stir in extra butter, egg yolks and rind until butter melts. Cool 10 minutes.

5 Spread filling over biscuit base, cover; refrigerate 2 hours.
6 Preheat oven to 240°C/475°F.
7 Beat egg whites in small bowl with electric mixer until soft peaks form; gradually add remaining sugar, 1 tablespoon at a time, beating until sugar dissolves between additions.
8 Roughen surface of filling with a fork before spreading with meringue. Spoon mixture into piping bag fitted with 1.5cm (½-inch) plain tube. Pipe meringue over filling. Bake about 5 minutes or until meringue is browned lightly.

prep + cook time 40 minutes (+ refrigeration)
serves 8
nutritional count per serving 23.2g total fat (13.9g saturated fat); 1914kJ (458 cal); 59.5g carbohydrate; 4.3g protein; 0.6g fibre

tip The base and filling can be made and assembled up to a day in advance. Meringue topping is best made just before serving. Roughing the surface of the filling will help the meringue to cling to the filling.

black-and-blue berry pie

400g (12½ ounces) frozen blackberries
⅓ cup (75g) caster (superfine) sugar
2 tablespoons cornflour (cornstarch)
2 tablespoons water
250g (8 ounces) fresh blueberries
2 teaspoons finely grated lemon rind
½ teaspoon mixed spice
1 egg white
2 teaspoons demerara sugar

CUSTARD PASTRY
1½ cups (225g) plain (all-purpose) flour
¼ cup (35g) cornflour (cornstarch)
¼ cup (30g) custard powder
2 tablespoons icing (confectioners') sugar
125g (4 ounces) cold butter, chopped coarsely
1 egg yolk
1 tablespoon iced water, approximately

1 Make custard pastry.
2 Meanwhile, combine 1 cup of the blackberries and sugar in medium saucepan. Bring to the boil. Blend cornflour with the water in small jug. Stir into berry mixture, stir over heat until mixture boils and thickens. Cool. Stir in remaining blackberries, blueberries, rind and spice.
3 Roll two-thirds of the pastry between sheets of baking paper until large enough to line 24cm (9½-inch) round loose-based flan tin. Ease pastry into tin; trim edge. Reserve and refrigerate excess pastry. Refrigerate pastry case 30 minutes.

4 Preheat oven to 200°C/400°F.
5 Spoon filling into pastry case. Brush edge with egg white. Roll reserved pastry between sheets of baking paper until large enough to cover pie. Cut into 10 x 1.5cm (½-inch) strips. Place strips over pie, weaving in and out to make lattice pattern. Trim edges, pressing to seal; sprinkle with demerara sugar.
6 Bake about 50 minutes or until browned. Stand 10 minutes before serving.

CUSTARD PASTRY Process flours, custard powder, icing sugar and butter until crumbly. Add egg yolk and enough of the water until ingredients just come together. Knead pastry on floured surface until smooth. Enclose in plastic wrap, refrigerate 30 minutes.

prep + cook time 1 hour 15 minutes
(+ refrigeration & cooling) serves 8
nutritional count per serving 14g total fat
(8.7g saturated fat); 1471kJ (352 cal);
49.9g carbohydrate; 4.9g protein; 4.8g fibre

walnut and toffeed fig tart

1 cup (250ml) pouring cream
¼ cup (60ml) milk
½ cup (110g) caster (superfine) sugar
2 teaspoons finely grated orange rind
2 eggs
⅓ cup (50g) wheaten cornflour (cornstarch)
½ cup (125ml) orange juice
80g (2½ ounces) butter, chopped coarsely
6 medium (350g) fresh figs, quartered

WALNUT PASTRY
⅓ cup (40g) walnuts
1 cup (150g) plain (all-purpose) flour
⅓ cup (55g) icing (confectioners') sugar
90g (3 ounces) cold butter, chopped coarsely
1 egg yolk
2 teaspoons iced water, approximately

TOFFEE
½ cup (110g) white sugar
¼ cup (60ml) water

1 To make custard, bring cream, milk, sugar and rind to the boil in medium saucepan. Whisk eggs in large bowl, whisk in sifted cornflour. Gradually whisk in hot milk mixture and juice. Return mixture to pan; stir over heat until mixture boils and thickens. Remove from heat; whisk in butter. Transfer to heatproof bowl; cover surface with plastic wrap, refrigerate about 2 hours or until cold.
2 Make walnut pastry.
3 Roll pastry between sheets of baking paper until large enough to line 11cm x 35cm (4½-inch x 14-inch) rectangular or 20cm (8-inch) round loose-based flan tin. Ease pastry into tin, pressing into base and sides; leave pastry overhanging edges. Place tin on oven tray; refrigerate 30 minutes.

4 Preheat oven to 180°C/350°F.
5 Line pastry with baking paper, fill with dried beans or rice. Bake 15 minutes; remove paper and beans. Bake 15 minutes, cool. Carefully trim pastry edge with a sharp knife.
6 Spoon custard into pastry case; top with figs.
7 Just before serving, make toffee.
8 Drizzle hot toffee over figs; stand 5 minutes before serving.

WALNUT PASTRY Process nuts until finely chopped. Add flour, icing sugar and butter; process until crumbly. Add egg yolk and most of the water, process until ingredients just come together. Knead on floured surface until smooth. Enclose in plastic wrap, refrigerate 1 hour.

TOFFEE Combine sugar and the water in small saucepan; stir without boiling until sugar is dissolved. Boil, uncovered, about 4 minutes or until caramel colour. Allow bubbles to subside.

prep + cook time 1 hour (+ cooling & refrigeration)
serves 8
nutritional count per serving 36.8g total fat (21.3g saturated fat); 2462kJ (589 cal); 59.7g carbohydrate; 6.5g protein; 2.3g fibre

tips We found wheaten cornflour gives a better texture to the custard, however, maize cornflour can also be used.
The toffee will begin to dissolve within 10 minutes of drizzling it over the figs, so it is best made just before serving.

whisky-laced fruit mince pies

⅓ cup (50g) raisins, chopped finely
¼ cup (40g) sultanas, chopped finely
¼ cup (40g) currants
1 small apple (130g), grated coarsely
⅓ cup (80ml) whisky
⅓ cup (75g) demerara sugar
1 teaspoon finely grated lemon rind
1 teaspoon ground cinnamon
40g (1½ ounces) frozen butter, grated coarsely
1 egg, beaten lightly
2 tablespoons demerara sugar, extra

CINNAMON PASTRY
1½ cups (225g) plain (all-purpose) flour
½ teaspoon ground cinnamon
125g (4 ounces) butter, chopped coarsely
1 egg

1 To make fruit mince, combine dried fruit, apple, whisky, sugar, rind and cinnamon in medium bowl. Cover; stand 48 hours. Stir in butter.
2 Make cinnamon pastry.
3 Preheat oven to 180°C/350°F. Grease 15 holes of two 12-hole (2 tablespoon/40ml) deep flat-based patty pans. Roll pastry between sheets of baking paper until large enough to line pans. Cut 15 x 7cm (2½-inch) rounds from pastry. Line pan holes with pastry, barely fill with fruit mince.
4 Cut 15 x 6cm (2¼-inch) rounds from pastry. Cut small rounds from centres of each round. Place over filling, press edges together. Brush pies with egg; sprinkle with extra sugar.
5 Bake pies about 30 minutes. Stand 5 minutes before transferring to a wire rack to cool.

CINNAMON PASTRY Process flour, cinnamon and butter until crumbly. Add egg; process until ingredients just come together. Knead dough on floured surface. Enclose with plastic wrap; refrigerate 30 minutes.

prep + cook time 1 hour
(+ standing & refrigeration) **makes** 15
nutritional count per serving 10g total fat
(6.2g saturated fat); 836kJ (200 cal);
24.9g carbohydrate; 2.8g protein; 1.1g fibre

pear and cinnamon sugar lattice pies

3 large pears (990g), peeled, cored, sliced thinly
¼ cup (55g) caster (superfine) sugar
2 teaspoons cornflour (cornstarch)
1 teaspoon vanilla extract
1 egg white
½ teaspoon ground cinnamon

PASTRY
1½ cups (225g) plain (all-purpose) flour
2 tablespoons icing (confectioners') sugar
125g (4 ounces) cold butter, chopped coarsely
1 egg yolk
2 tablespoons iced water, approximately

1 Make pastry.
2 Grease four 10cm (4-inch) round loose-based flan
tins. Divide pastry into five portions. Roll each of
four portions between baking paper until large
enough to line tins. Lift pastry into tins, press into
sides; trim edges. Reserve pastry scraps with the
fifth portion. Refrigerate 30 minutes.
3 Preheat oven to 180°C/350°F.
4 Meanwhile, combine pear and one-third of the
sugar in medium saucepan. Cook, covered, until pear
is tender. Drain, reserve 1 tablespoon liquid. Blend or
process mixture until almost smooth. Return to pan
with half the remaining sugar. Blend cornflour with
reserved liquid; stir into pear mixture; stir over heat
until mixture boils and thickens. Stir in extract; cool.
5 Spoon pear filling into pastry cases. Brush edges
with egg white. Roll all reserved pastry between
sheets of baking paper. Cut into 12 x 1cm (½-inch)
strips. Weave strips over pies. Trim edges, pressing
to seal; sprinkle with combined remaining sugar
and cinnamon. Bake about 50 minutes.

PASTRY Process flour, icing sugar and butter until
crumbly. Add egg yolk and enough of the water to
make ingredients just come together. Knead dough
on floured surface until smooth. Enclose in plastic
wrap; refrigerate 30 minutes.

prep + cook time 1 hour 15 minutes (+ refrigeration)
makes 4
nutritional count per serving 27.9g total fat
(17.5g saturated fat); 2400kj (574cal);
86.1g carbohydrate; 8.5g protein; 5.6g fibre

spiced apple parcels

50g (1½ ounces) butter
3 medium apples (450g), peeled, cored,
   chopped finely
2 tablespoons maple syrup
1 tablespoon caster (superfine) sugar
½ teaspoon mixed spice
¼ cup (40g) sultanas
¼ cup (35g) slivered almonds, toasted
1½ sheets butter puff pastry
1 egg, beaten lightly

1   Melt butter in large frying pan; cook apple,
stirring occasionally, about 5 minutes or until
browned lightly. Add maple syrup, sugar and spice;
cook, stirring, about 5 minutes or until liquid boils
and caramelises. Transfer to medium heatproof
bowl. Stir in sultanas and nuts. Cool 20 minutes.

2   Meanwhile, preheat oven to 220°C/ 425°F.
3   Cut whole pastry sheet in quarters; cut half sheet
in half. Spoon ¼ cup apple mixture along one half
of pastry squares. Fold over to form rectangles,
pressing edges to seal with a fork. Brush with egg.
Make three slits in parcels.
4   Bake about 20 minutes or until browned.

prep + cook time 45 minutes (+ cooling) **makes** 6
nutritional count per serving 20.5g total fat
(10.1g saturated fat); 1446kJ (346 cal);
35.4g carbohydrate; 5g protein; 2.4g fibre

serving suggestion Dust with sifted icing sugar
and serve with ice-cream.

apple and mixed berry fillo pie

6 medium apples (900g), peeled, cored, sliced thinly
¼ cup (55g) caster (superfine) sugar
2 teaspoons cornflour (cornstarch)
2 teaspoons water
2 teaspoons vanilla extract
½ teaspoon ground cinnamon
300g (9½ ounces) frozen mixed berries
4 sheets fillo pastry
30g (1 ounce) butter, melted
¼ teaspoon ground cinnamon, extra
2 tablespoons flaked almonds

1 Preheat oven to 220°C/ 425°F. Grease 1-litre (4-cup) pie dish.
2 Combine apple and sugar in large saucepan. Bring to the boil; simmer, covered, about 8 minutes or until tender.
3 Blend cornflour with the water in small jug, stir into apple mixture with extract and cinnamon; stir gently over heat until mixture boils and thickens slightly. Stir in berries, spoon into dish.
4 Brush each sheet of pastry with butter. Scrunch and place over filling. Sprinkle with extra cinnamon and nuts.
5 Bake pie about 20 minutes until browned.

prep + cook time 45 minutes **serves** 6
nutritional count per serving 6.4g total fat (2.9g saturated fat); 681kJ (163 cal); 31.7g carbohydrate; 2.7g protein; 5.6g fibre

pumpkin and sweet potato pie

250g (8 ounces) coarsely chopped pumpkin
250g (8 ounces) coarsely chopped kumara
  (orange sweet potato)
½ cup (110g) firmly packed light brown sugar
1 teaspoon vanilla extract
1 teaspoon ground cinnamon
½ teaspoon each ground ginger and nutmeg
1 cup (250ml) pouring cream
2 eggs

PASTRY
1½ cups (225g) plain (all-purpose) flour
2 tablespoons icing (confectioners') sugar
125g (4 ounces) cold butter, chopped coarsely
1 egg yolk
2 tablespoons iced water, approximately

MAPLE CREAM
1 cup (250ml) thickened (heavy) cream
2 tablespoons maple syrup

1 Make pastry. Grease 24cm (9½-inch) round loose-based flan tin.
2 Roll pastry between sheets of baking paper until large enough to line tin. Lift pastry into tin, press into side; trim edge. Refrigerate 20 minutes.
3 Preheat oven to 200°C/400°F. Place tin on oven tray; line pastry with baking paper, fill with dried beans or rice. Bake 10 minutes. Remove paper and beans; bake 10 minutes. Cool.
4 Reduce oven to 180°C/350°F.
5 Meanwhile, steam pumpkin and kumara, separately, until tender. Cool 10 minutes.
6 Blend or process pumpkin and kumara with remaining ingredients until smooth. Pour mixture into pastry case. Bake about 1 hour or until filling is set. Cool. Refrigerate until filling is firm.
7 Serve with maple cream.

PASTRY Process flour, icing sugar and butter until crumbly. Add egg yolk and enough of the water to make ingredients just come together. Knead dough on floured surface until smooth. Enclose dough with plastic wrap; refrigerate 30 minutes.

MAPLE CREAM Beat cream and syrup in small bowl with electric mixer until soft peaks form.

prep + cook time 1 hour 30 minutes
(+ refrigeration) serves 8
nutritional count per serving 40.5g total fat
(25.8g saturated fat); 2454kJ (587 cal);
49.2g carbohydrate; 7.7g protein; 2g fibre

tips It is important to steam, not boil, the pumpkin and kumara, to prevent vegetables becoming watery. Chop vegetables the same size so they cook evenly.

white chocolate, lime and ginger mousse tarts

90g (3 ounces) white eating chocolate,
  chopped coarsely
1 egg yolk
3 teaspoons finely grated lime rind
⅔ cup (160ml) thickened (heavy) cream, whipped

GINGER PASTRY
1½ cups (225g) plain (all-purpose) flour
2 tablespoons icing (confectioners') sugar
1 teaspoon ground ginger
125g (4 ounces) cold butter, chopped coarsely
1 egg yolk
2 tablespoons iced water, approximately

1 Make ginger pastry. Grease 10 x 8cm (3¼-inch)
round loose-based flan tins.
2 Divide pastry into 10 portions, roll each between
sheets of baking paper until large enough to line
tins. Lift pastry into tins. Press into sides; trim
edges. Prick bases with fork, place on oven trays.
Refrigerate 20 minutes.
3 Meanwhile, preheat oven to 200°C/400°F.
4 Bake pastry cases 20 minutes. Cool.
5 Melt chocolate in medium heatproof bowl
over medium saucepan of simmering water. Cool
10 minutes. Stir in egg yolk and rind; fold in cream.
6 Spoon chocolate mousse mixture into pastry
cases. Refrigerate 2 hours or until firm.

GINGER PASTRY Process flour, icing sugar,
ginger and butter until crumbly. Add egg yolk
and enough of the water to make ingredients just
come together. Knead dough on floured surface
until smooth. Enclose with plastic wrap; refrigerate
30 minutes.

prep + cook time 45 minutes
(+ refrigeration & cooling) makes 10
nutritional count per serving 20.5g total fat
(12.9g saturated fat); 1241kJ (297 cal);
23.9g carbohydrate; 4.5g protein; 0.9g fibre

caramel pecan pie

½ cup (175g) golden syrup (or treacle)
¼ cup (55g) firmly packed light brown sugar
2 eggs, beaten lightly
50g (1½ ounces) butter, melted
2 tablespoons plain (all-purpose) flour
2 teaspoons vanilla extract
1 cup pecans (120g), toasted, halved

PASTRY
1½ cups (225g) plain (all-purpose) flour
2 tablespoons icing (confectioners') sugar
125g (4 ounces) cold butter, chopped coarsely
1 egg yolk
2 tablespoons iced water, approximately

1 Make pastry.
2 Roll pastry between sheets of baking paper until large enough to line 24cm (9½-inch) round loose-based flan tin. Ease pastry into tin, press into base and side; trim edge. Refrigerate 30 minutes.
3 Preheat oven to 200°C/400°F.
4 Place tin on oven tray. Line pastry with baking paper; fill with dried beans or rice. Bake 10 minutes; remove paper and beans. Bake 10 minutes; cool.
5 Reduce oven to 180°C/350°F.
6 Combine syrup, sugar, eggs, butter, flour and extract in small bowl; whisk until smooth. Pour mixture into pastry case; top with nuts.
7 Bake pie about 40 minutes or until set; cool.

PASTRY Process flour, icing sugar and butter until crumbly. Add egg yolk and enough of the water to make ingredients just come together. Knead dough on floured surface until smooth. Enclose with plastic wrap; refrigerate 30 minutes.

prep + cook time 1 hour 20 minutes
(+ refrigeration) **serves** 8
nutritional count per serving 31.1g total fat
(13.2g saturated fat); 2094kJ (501 cal);
49g carbohydrate; 7.1g protein; 2.4g fibre

chocolate orange ricotta tarts

1½ cups (360g) ricotta cheese
½ cup (110g) caster (superfine) sugar
1 egg, beaten lightly
90g (3 ounces) finely chopped dark
 (semi-sweet) eating chocolate
⅓ cup (50g) finely chopped glacé orange
¼ cup (40g) sultanas
3 sheets butter puff pastry
1 tablespoon milk
1 tablespoon icing (confectioners') sugar

1 Preheat oven to 200°C/400°F. Line oven trays
with baking paper.
2 Combine cheese, sugar and egg in medium
bowl. Stir in chocolate and fruit.

3 Cut 12 x 11cm (4½-inch) rounds from pastry;
place rounds on trays. Divide ricotta mixture
among rounds, leaving a 2.5cm (1-inch) border.
Fold pastry edge up. Brush pastry with milk; bake
tarts about 12 minutes or until browned. Cool
5 minutes before dusting with sifted icing sugar.

prep + cook time 35 minutes makes 12
nutritional count per serving 15.7g total fat
(9.5g saturated fat); 1129kJ (270 cal);
35g carbohydrate; 6.5g protein; 1.1g fibre

coconut and passionfruit custard pie

½ cup (75g) plain (all-purpose) flour
1 cup (220g) caster (superfine) sugar
1 cup (80g) desiccated coconut
4 eggs, beaten lightly
2 teaspoons vanilla extract
125g (4 ounces) butter, melted
1⅓ cups (330ml) milk
½ cup (125ml) passionfruit pulp
1 tablespoon icing (confectioners') sugar

1 Preheat oven to 200°C/400°F. Grease straight-sided 24cm (9½-inch) pie dish.
2 Sift flour into large bowl; stir in remaining ingredients; pour into dish.
3 Bake pie about 1 hour or until set.
4 Serve dusted with sifted icing sugar.

prep + cook time 1 hour 10 minutes **serves** 8
nutritional count per serving 23.8g total fat (15.6g saturated fat); 1647kJ (394 cal); 38.1g carbohydrate; 7g protein; 4.1g fibre

tips You will need about six passionfruit for this recipe. The base of this pie will develop a layer of custard during the baking.
serving suggestion Serve with whipped cream or ice-cream.

little salty caramel meringue pies

395g (12½ ounces) canned sweetened
  condensed milk
30g (1 ounce) butter
¼ cup (90g) golden syrup (or treacle)
2 teaspoons sea salt flakes
¼ cup (60ml) pouring cream

PASTRY
1 cup (150g) plain (all-purpose) flour
⅓ cup (55g) icing (confectioners') sugar
90g (3 ounces) butter, chopped coarsely
1 egg yolk
1 tablespoon iced water, approximately

MERINGUE
4 egg whites
1 cup (220g) caster (superfine) sugar

1 Make pastry.
2 Divide pastry into eight portions. Roll one
portion at a time between sheets of baking paper
until large enough to line eight 8cm (3-inch) loose-
based flan tins. Ease pastry into tins, pressing into
base and side; trim edges. prick bases with fork.
Place on oven tray; refrigerate 20 minutes.
3 Meanwhile, preheat oven to 180°C/350°F.
4 Line pastry with baking paper, fill with dried
beans or rice. Bake 10 minutes; remove paper and
beans. Bake about 5 minutes or until browned; cool.
5 Combine condensed milk, butter, syrup and salt
in small heavy-based saucepan; stir over medium
heat about 12 minutes or until caramel-coloured.
Stir in cream. Spread filling into pastry cases.
6 Make meringue.
7 Spoon meringue onto tarts. Bake tarts about
5 minutes or until browned lightly.

PASTRY Process flour, icing sugar and butter until
crumbly. Add egg yolk and most of the water;
process until ingredients just come together. Knead
pastry on floured surface until smooth. Enclose with
plastic wrap; refrigerate 30 minutes.

MERINGUE Beat egg whites in small bowl with
electric mixer until soft peaks form. Add sugar
gradually, beating until dissolved between
each addition.

prep + cook time 1 hour (+ refrigeration) makes 8
nutritional count per serving 17.9g total fat
(11.4g saturated fat); 2195kJ (525 cal);
85.2g carbohydrate; 9.1g protein; 0.7g fibre

old-fashioned apple and rhubarb pie

5 large (1kg) apples, sliced thickly
⅓ cup (75g) caster (superfine) sugar
½ cup (125ml) water
1 vanilla bean, split
500g (1 pound) trimmed rhubarb,
  chopped coarsely
1 tablespoon lemon juice
1 egg, beaten lightly
1 teaspoon white sugar

ALMOND PASTRY
2½ cups (375g) plain (all-purpose) flour
½ cup (60g) ground almonds
1 cup (160g) icing (confectioners') sugar
250g (8 ounces) cold butter, chopped coarsely
2 egg yolks
1 tablespoon iced water

1 Combine apple, caster sugar, the water and half the vanilla bean in large saucepan, cover, bring to the boil. Simmer about 10 minutes or until apple is tender. Stir in rhubarb, cover, simmer about 3 minutes or until rhubarb is soft. Drain well, place apple mixture in medium bowl; stir in lemon juice. Cool.
2 Make almond pastry.
3 Preheat oven to 180°C/350°F.
4 Roll two thirds of the pastry between sheets of baking paper until large enough to line deep 24cm (9½-inch) pie dish. Lift pastry into dish; press into base and side, trim edge. Refrigerate 30 minutes.

5 Line pastry with baking paper, cover with dried beans or rice. Place on oven tray. Bake 15 minutes; remove paper and beans, bake about 15 minutes or until browned; cool.
6 Spoon apple mixture into pastry case. Roll remaining pastry between sheets of baking paper until large enough to cover pie dish. Brush edge of pastry case with egg. Place pastry over pie; pinch edge of pastry, trim edge. Cut out 2.5cm (1-inch) round from centre of pie. Brush pastry with egg, sprinkle with white sugar. Bake about 35 minutes or until browned. Stand 10 minutes before serving.

ALMOND PASTRY Scrape seeds from remaining half of vanilla bean. Process flour, ground almonds, icing sugar and butter until crumbly. Add egg yolks, vanilla seeds and most of the water; process until ingredients just come together. Knead on floured surface until smooth. Enclose with plastic wrap; refrigerate 30 minutes.

prep + cook time 4 hours
(+ cooling & refrigeration) serves 8
nutritional count per serving 14.4g total fat
(3.6g saturated fat); 1910kJ (457 cal);
75.7g carbohydrate; 13.5g protein; 5.5g fibre

serving suggestion Serve the pie with cream, ice-cream or custard.

vanilla custard pie

2 sheets puff pastry
2 tablespoons icing (confectioners') sugar
¼ cup (20g) flaked almonds
1 cup (220g) caster (superfine) sugar
1 cup (150g) cornflour (cornstarch)
½ cup (60g) custard powder
1¼ cups (300ml) thickened (heavy) cream
3½ cups (875ml) milk
1 vanilla bean
60g (2 ounces) butter, chopped coarsely
2 egg yolks

1 Preheat oven to 220°C/425°F. Grease 24cm (9½-inch) round springform tin. Line oven trays with baking paper.
2 Place pastry sheets on oven trays; brush with a little water. Sprinkle evenly with sifted icing sugar. Sprinkle one pastry sheet with nuts. Bake about 15 minutes or until browned lightly. Gently flatten pastry with egg slice. Cut each sheet into 24cm (9½-inch) rounds. Place plain sheet in tin.
3 Meanwhile, combine caster sugar, cornflour and custard powder in medium saucepan. Combine cream and milk in large jug. Gradually stir milk mixture into sugar mixture, until smooth.
4 Halve vanilla bean lengthways, scrape seeds into pan; add butter. Bring to the boil, stirring constantly until mixture boils and thickens. Simmer about 3 minutes, strring constantly. Remove from heat; stir in egg yolks. Spread mixture over pastry in tin. Top with remaining round, nut side up. Refrigerate, 2 hours or until firm.
5 Serve dusted with a little extra sifted icing sugar.

prep + cook time 40 minutes (+ refrigeration)
serves 10
nutritional count per serving 29.4g total fat (13.8g saturated fat); 2178kJ (521 cal); 59g carbohydrate; 6.6g protein; 0.7g fibre

passionfruit curd and coconut tarts

1 cup (80g) desiccated coconut
1 egg white, beaten lightly
2 tablespoons caster (superfine) sugar
¼ cup (60ml) thickened (heavy) cream, whipped
1 tablespoon passionfruit pulp

PASSIONFRUIT CURD
½ cup (125ml) passionfruit pulp
½ teaspoon finely grated lemon rind
1 tablespoon lemon juice
½ cup (110g) caster (superfine) sugar
80g (2½ ounces) butter, chopped coarsely
1 egg, beaten lightly
1 egg yolk

1 Make passionfruit curd.
2 Preheat oven to 150°C/300°F. Grease 12-hole (2-tablespoon/40ml) mini muffin pan.
3 Combine coconut, egg white and sugar in bowl. Press mixture firmly and evenly over bases and sides of pan holes. Bake about 20 minutes or until browned lightly. Cool.
4 Fold cream into ½ cup of the passionfruit curd. Reserve remaining curd for another use.
5 Divide passionfruit mixture among coconut cases; top each with a little passionfruit pulp.

PASSIONFRUIT CURD Press passionfruit firmly through a sieve over a small bowl. You will need ¼ cup passionfruit juice for this recipe. Combine passionfruit juice with remaining ingredients in medium heatproof bowl. Stir over a medium saucepan of simmering water until the mixture thickly coats the back of a wooden spoon, about 10 minutes. Cool; refrigerate 2 hours or until cold.

prep + cook time 1 hour 15 minutes
(+ cooling & refrigeration) **makes** 12
nutritional count per serving 12.6g total fat
(8.6g saturated fat); 744kJ (178 cal);
13.4g carbohydrate; 2.1g protein; 2.7g fibre

tips You will need about six passionfruit for this recipe. Remaining passionfruit curd is delicious on scones, in pavlovas or meringues.

rhubarb pies with meringue topping

1 bunch fresh rhubarb (350g trimmed)
1 tablespoon caster (superfine) sugar
2 sheets shortcrust pastry
2 egg whites
½ cup (110g) caster (superfine) sugar, extra
1 tablespoon flaked almonds, chopped coarsely

1   Preheat oven to 200°C/400°F. Grease 12-hole (1½-tablespoon/30ml) shallow round-based patty pans.
2   Chop rhubarb into 2cm (¾-inch) cubes. Spread rhubarb onto baking-paper-lined oven tray; sprinkle with sugar. Bake, uncovered, about 10 minutes or until tender; cool.
3   Cut 12 x 7cm (2½-inch) rounds from pastry. Press rounds into pan holes; prick bases with fork. Refrigerate 20 minutes.

4   Bake pastry cases 10 minutes; cool.
5   Beat egg whites in small bowl with electric mixer until soft peaks form; gradually add extra sugar, beating until sugar dissolves.
6   Divide rhubarb filling among pastry cases. Spoon meringue over filling; sprinkle with nuts. Bake about 5 minutes or until browned lightly. Stand 5 minutes before serving.

prep + cook time 55 minutes (+ cooling & refrigeration) **makes** 12
nutritional count per serving 9.1g total fat (4.1g saturated fat); 794kJ (190 cal); 23.5g carbohydrate; 3.3g protein; 1.4g fibre

tip You can use one quantity shortcrust pastry (page 4) instead of the store-bought pastry sheets.

french apple quince tarts

1 sheet butter puff pastry
50g (1½ ounces) quince paste
2 tablespoons water
2 small (260g) apples, peeled

1 Preheat oven to 200°C/400°F. Line large oven tray with baking paper.
2 Cut four 11cm (4½-inch) rounds from pastry; place on tray about 3cm (1 inch) apart. Heat paste with the water in small saucepan until smooth. Brush pastry with some of the quince mixture.

3 Quarter and core apples; slice thinly. Overlap slices on pastry. Brush apple with a little more quince mixture. Bake about 20 minutes or until pastry is crisp and apple is tender.
4 Brush tarts with remaining quince mixture; serve tarts warm.

prep + cook time 40 minutes **serves** 4
nutritional count per serving 9.5g total fat
(5.1g saturated fat); 798kJ (191 cal);
23.1g carbohydrate; 2.5g protein; 2.1g fibre

tip Choose small apples – golden delicious or granny smith are best so they will fit on the small pastry rounds neatly.
serving suggestion Serve with vanilla ice-cream.

turkish delight rosewater tarts

250g (8 ounces) small strawberries, quartered
50g (1½ ounces) rose turkish delight,
  chopped coarsely
2 tablespoons pistachios, chopped coarsely
2 tablespoons dried pink rose petals
½ cup (10g) rose persian fairy floss

PISTACHIO PASTRY
¼ cup (35g) shelled pistachios
1¼ cups (185g) plain (all-purpose) flour
½ cup (80g) icing (confectioners') sugar
125g (4 ounces) butter, chopped coarsely
2 egg yolks
2 teaspoons iced water, approximately

MASCARPONE FILLING
250g (8 ounces) mascarpone
½ cup (80g) icing (confectioners') sugar
2 teaspoons rosewater
100g (3 ounces) rose turkish delight,
  chopped coarsely
½ cup (125ml) thickened (heavy) cream

1 Make pistachio pastry.
2 Preheat oven to 180°C/350°F.
3 Divide pastry into six portions. Roll one portion at a time between sheets of baking paper until large enough to line six deep 9cm (3½-inch) flan tins. Ease pastry into tins, pressing over base and side; trim edges, prick bases with fork. Place tins on oven tray; refrigerate 30 minutes.
4 Line pastry with baking paper, fill with dried beans or rice. Bake 15 minutes; remove paper and beans. Bake further 15 minutes or until pastry is lightly browned; cool.
5 Meanwhile, make mascarpone filling.
6 Divide mascarpone filling among pastry cases. Top with strawberries, turkish delight, nuts, rose petals and fairy floss.

PISTACHIO PASTRY Process nuts until chopped finely. Add flour, icing sugar and butter; process until crumbly. Add egg yolks and enough of the water to make ingredients just come together. Knead on floured surface until smooth. Enclose with plastic wrap; refrigerate 30 minutes.

MASCARPONE FILLING Combine mascarpone, icing sugar, rosewater and turkish delight in a medium bowl. Beat cream in small bowl with electric mixer until soft peaks form; fold into mascarpone mixture.

prep + cook time 55 minutes (+ refrigeration)
serves 6
nutritional count per serving 57.3g total fat (33.5g saturated fat); 3494kJ (836 cal); 73.4g carbohydrate; 8.8g protein; 3.2g fibre

tips Rosewater varies in strengths depending on the brand; add it gradually to taste. Persian fairy floss is usually labelled pashmak and is available from specialty food stores.

strawberry and lemon curd tart

250g (8 ounces) fresh strawberries, quartered
1 tablespoon icing (confectioners') sugar

LEMON CURD
3 eggs
3 egg yolks
1 cup (220g) caster (superfine) sugar
125g (4 ounces) butter, chopped coarsely
½ cup (125ml) lemon juice

SOUR CREAM PASTRY
1½ cups (225g) plain (all-purpose) flour
1 tablespoon caster (superfine) sugar
75g (2½ ounces) butter, chopped coarsely
⅓ cup (80g) sour cream
2 teaspoons iced water, approximately

1 Make lemon curd and sour cream pastry.
2 Preheat oven to 200°C/400°F. Grease 24cm (9½-inch) loose-based flan tin.
3 Roll pastry between sheets of baking paper until large enough to line tin. Lift pastry into tin, ease into base and side; trim edge. Refrigerate 30 minutes. Bake pastry case 25 minutes; cool.
4 Spoon lemon curd into pastry case; top with strawberries. Serve dusted with sifted icing sugar.

LEMON CURD Whisk eggs, egg yolks and sugar in medium bowl until combined. Melt butter with juice in small saucepan over low heat; bring to the boil, gradually whisk into egg mixture. Return mixture to pan, whisk over low heat about 10 minutes or until thick; cool. Transfer to small bowl, cover, refrigerate overnight.

SOUR CREAM PASTRY Process flour, sugar and butter until crumbly. Add sour cream and enough of the water to make ingredients just come together. Knead dough on floured surface until smooth. Wrap in plastic; refrigerate 30 minutes.

prep + cook time 55 minutes (+ refrigeration)
serves 10
nutritional count per serving 23.2g total fat (14g saturated fat); 1321kJ (316 cal); 42.4g carbohydrate; 6.2g protein; 1.4g fibre

raspberry almond crumble tart

1½ cups (225g) frozen raspberries
1 teaspoon icing (confectioners') sugar

ALMOND CRUMBLE PASTRY
150g (5 ounces) butter, softened
1 teaspoon vanilla extract
⅔ cup (150g) caster (superfine) sugar
1 egg
½ cup (60g) ground almonds
1½ cups (225g) plain (all-purpose) flour

1   Make almond crumble pastry.
2   Roll two-thirds of the pastry between sheets of baking paper until large enough to line 11cm x 35cm (4½-inch x 14-inch) rectangular loose-based flan tin. Lift pastry into tin, press into base and sides; trim edge. Prick pastry base with fork; refrigerate 30 minutes. Reserve remaining pastry.
3   Meanwhile, preheat oven to 200°C/400°F.
4   Place tin on oven tray; bake, about 10 minutes or until browned lightly. Sprinkle raspberries over base, sprinkle with remaining crumbled pastry. Bake further 20 minutes or until well browned; cool in pan.
5   Dust with sifted icing sugar before serving.

ALMOND CRUMBLE PASTRY   Beat butter in small bowl with electric mixer until smooth. Add extract, sugar and egg; beat until combined. Stir in ground almonds and half the flour. Work in remaining flour using hand. Knead pastry on floured surface until smooth. Enclose with plastic wrap; refrigerate 30 minutes.

prep + cook time 1 hour (+ refrigeration & cooling)
serves 8
nutritional count per serving 20.6g total fat (10.7g saturated fat); 1576kJ (377 cal); 41.5g carbohydrate; 5.8g protein; 3.2g fibre

tip   This recipe is best made on day of serving as the raspberries will soften the pastry.
serving suggestion   Serve with thick (double) cream, ice-cream or custard.

raspberry and chocolate tart

250g (8 ounces) fresh raspberries,
  mashed lightly
1¼ cups (310ml) pouring cream
200g (6½ ounces) dark (semi-sweet) eating
  chocolate, chopped coarsely
2 eggs, beaten lightly

CHOCOLATE ALMOND PASTRY
1½ cups (225g) plain (all-purpose) flour
¼ cup (30g) ground almonds
2 tablespoons caster (superfine) sugar
2 tablespoons cocoa powder
125g (4 ounces) cold butter, chopped coarsely
1 egg

1 Make chocolate almond pastry.
2 Preheat oven to 200°C/400°F. Grease 11cm x
35cm (4-inch x 14-inch) rectangular loose-based
flan tin.
3 Roll pastry between sheets of baking paper
until large enough to line tin. Lift pastry into tin,
ease into base and side; trim edge. Refrigerate
30 minutes.

4 Bake pastry case about 15 minutes or until
browned; cool. Reduce oven to 180°C/350°F.
5 Spoon raspberries into pastry case. Heat cream,
remove from heat, stir in chocolate. Stir eggs into
chocolate mixture, gently pour over raspberries.
6 Bake tart about 25 minutes or until set. Cool;
refrigerate tart for at least 3 hours or overnight.

CHOCOLATE ALMOND PASTRY Process flour,
ground almonds, sugar, cocoa and butter until
crumbly. Add egg; process until ingredients just
come together. Knead dough on floured surface
until smooth. Enclose with plastic wrap; refrigerate
pastry 30 minutes.

prep + cook time 1 hour
(+ refrigeration & cooling) serves 6
nutritional count per serving 55.9g total fat
(36.5g saturated fat); 3252kJ (778 cal);
56.6g carbohydrate; 11.8g protein; 5.8g fibre

prune and port tart

1 cup (200g) seeded prunes
250g (8 ounces) crème fraîche
2 eggs
2 tablespoons caster (superfine) sugar
2 tablespoons port
1 tablespoon cornflour (cornstarch)
½ teaspoon garam masala
1 tablespoon icing (confectioners') sugar

WALNUT PASTRY
1¼ cups (185g) plain (all-purpose) flour
½ cup (50g) walnuts
2 tablespoons caster (superfine) sugar
125g (4 ounces) butter, chopped coarsely
1 egg

1   Make walnut pastry.
2   Preheat oven to 200°C/400°F. Grease 24cm
(9½-inch) loose-based flan tin.
3   Roll pastry between sheets of baking paper until

4   Lift pastry into tin; ease into base and side, trim
edge. Refrigerate 20 minutes. Place pastry case on
oven tray, bake 20 minutes; cool. Reduce oven to
180°C/350°F.
5   Place prunes into pastry case. Combine crème
fraîche, eggs, sugar, port, cornflour and garam
masala in large jug; gently pour over prunes.
6   Bake about 25 minutes or until custard is set;
cool. Refrigerate overnight. Dust with sifted
icing sugar.

WALNUT PASTRY   Process flour, nuts and sugar
until combined. Add butter; process until crumbly.
Add egg, process until ingredients just come
together. Knead on floured surface until smooth.
Enclose with plastic wrap; refrigerate 30 minutes.

prep + cook time 1 hour (+ refrigeration & cooling)
serves 8
nutritional count per serving 31.9g total fat

peach jalousie

2 sheets puff pastry
500g (16 ounces) peaches, sliced thinly
1 tablespoon lemon juice
1 egg, beaten lightly
2 teaspoons demerara sugar

FRANGIPANE
60g (2 ounces) butter
1 teaspoon vanilla extract
¼ cup (55g) caster (superfine) sugar
1 egg
⅔ cup (80g) ground almonds
1 tablespoon plain (all-purpose) flour

1 Make frangipane.
2 Preheat oven to 200°C/400°F. Line oven tray with baking paper.
3 Cut pastry sheets in half. Place two halves on tray. Spread with frangipane, leaving a 2cm (¾-inch) border. Top with peach slices, brush with lemon juice. Gently fold remaining pastry in half lengthways. Cut through folded edge of pastry at 1.5cm (½-inch) intervals, leaving a 2cm (¾-inch) border on three open sides. Carefully unfold cut pastry strip, place over peaches. Press edges of pastry together. Brush pastry with egg; sprinkle with sugar. Bake jalousie about 20 minutes or until pastry is browned.
4 Stand jalousie 10 minutes before serving.

FRANGIPANE Beat butter, extract and sugar in small bowl with electric mixer until creamy. Beat in egg until combined; stir in ground almonds and flour.

prep + cook time 3 hours (+ cooling) serves 8
nutritional count per serving 22.5g total fat (5.5g saturated fat); 1421kJ (340 cal); 27.3g carbohydrate; 6.6g protein; 2.1g fibre

Nectarines, apricots or berries would be delicious in place of the peaches. **serving suggestion** Serve with thick (double) cream.

glossary

ALLSPICE also called pimento or jamaican pepper; like a combination of nutmeg, cumin, clove and cinnamon. Available whole or ground.

BAKING PAPER also known as parchment paper or baking parchment – is a silicone-coated paper that is primarily used for lining baking pans and oven trays so cakes and biscuits won't stick, making removal easy.

BUTTER we use salted butter unless stated otherwise; 125g is equal to 1 stick (4 ounces).

CAJUN SEASONING used to give an authentic USA Deep South spicy cajun flavour to food, this packaged blend of assorted herbs and spices can include paprika, basil, onion, fennel, thyme, cayenne and tarragon.

CAPERS the grey-green buds of a warm climate (usually Mediterranean) shrub, sold either dried and salted or pickled in a vinegar brine; tiny young ones, called baby capers, are also available both in brine or dried in salt. Their pungent taste adds piquancy to a tapenade, sauces and condiments.

CAPSICUM also called pepper or bell pepper. Discard seeds and membranes before use.

CHEESE
blue mould-treated cheeses mottled with blue veining. Varieties include firm and crumbly stilton types and mild, creamy brie-like cheeses.
brie soft-ripened cow-milk cheese with a delicate, creamy texture and a rich, sweet taste that varies from buttery to mushroomy.
cheddar is a relatively hard, yellow to off-white, and sometimes sharp cheese originally made in the English village of Cheddar, in Somerset.
fetta Greek in origin; a crumbly textured goat- or sheep-milk cheese having a sharp, salty taste. Ripened and stored in salted whey; particularly good cubed and tossed into salads.
manchego white to ivory cheese of Spanish origin usually made from sheep's milk.
parmesan also called parmigiano; is a hard, grainy cow's milk cheese

originating in the Parma region of Italy. The curd for this cheese is salted in brine for a month, then aged for up to two years in humid conditions. Reggiano is the best parmesan, aged for a minimum two years and made in the Italian region of Emilia-Romagna.
pecorino the Italian generic name for cheeses made from sheep milk. This family of hard, white to pale-yellow cheeses has been matured for eight to 12 months. It's classified according to the area in which it is produced – romano from Rome, sardo from Sardinia, siciliano from Sicily and toscano from Tuscany. If you can't find pecorino, use parmesan.
pizza cheese a blend of varying proportions of processed grated mozzarella, cheddar and parmesan.

CHICKEN
breast fillet breast halved, skinned and boned.
tenderloin thin strip of meat from under the breast; good for stir-frying.
thigh fillet thigh with skin and centre bone removed.

CHICKPEAS also called garbanzos, hummus or channa; an irregularly round, sandy-coloured legume used extensively in Mediterranean, Indian and Hispanic cooking. Firm texture even after cooking with a floury mouth-feel and robust nutty flavour. Buy canned or dried (reconstitute for several hours in cold water before use).

CHINESE COOKING WINE also called shao hsing or chinese rice wine; made from fermented rice, wheat, sugar and salt with a 13.5 per cent alcohol content. Inexpensive and found in Asian food shops; if you can't find it, replace with mirin or sherry.

CHIVES related to the onion and leek; has a subtle onion flavour. Used more for flavour than as an ingredient; chopped finely, used in sauces, dressings, omelettes or as a garnish.

CHORIZO sausage of Spanish origin, made of coarsely ground pork and seasoned with garlic and chilli. They are deeply smoked, very spicy and available fresh or dry-cured.

CINNAMON available both in the piece (called sticks or quills) and ground into powder; one of the world's most common spices, used universally as a sweet, fragrant flavouring for both sweet and savoury foods. The dried inner bark of the shoots of the Sri Lankan native cinnamon tree; much of what is sold as the real thing is in fact cassia, Chinese cinnamon, from the cassia tree.

CORIANDER also called cilantro, pak chee or chinese parsley; bright-green-leafed herb with both pungent aroma and taste. Often stirred into or sprinkled over a dish just before serving for maximum impact as, like other leafy herbs, its characteristics diminish with cooking. Coriander seeds are dried and sold either whole or ground, and neither form tastes remotely like the fresh leaf.

CORNFLOUR also known as cornstarch. Available made from corn or wheat (wheaten cornflour gives a lighter texture in cakes); used as a thickening agent in cooking.

CREAM we used fresh cream, also known as pure or pouring cream unless otherwise stated. Contains no additives. The minimum fat content is 35 per cent.
crème fraîche a mature, naturally fermented cream (minimum fat content 35 per cent) with a velvety texture and slightly tangy, nutty flavour. This French variation of sour cream, can boil without curdling and be used in sweet and savoury dishes.
sour a thick, commercially cultured sour cream with a minimum fat content of 35 per cent.
thick (double) a dolloping cream with minimum fat content of 45 per cent.
thickened (heavy) a whipping cream containing thickener. Minimum fat content 35 per cent.

CUMIN also known as zeera or comino; resembling caraway in size, cumin is the dried seed of a plant related to the parsley family. Its spicy, almost curry-like flavour is essential to the traditional foods of Mexico, India,

North Africa and the Middle East. Available dried as seeds or ground. Black cumin seeds are smaller than standard cumin, and dark brown rather than true black; they are mistakenly confused with kalonji (black onion seeds).

CURRY PASTES
balti combines herbs and spices such as coriander, cumin, turmeric, chilli, pepper and garlic.
butter chicken A mildly spiced rich paste from the North Indian state of Punjab. The combination of tomato and fenugreek leaves gives the paste its distinctive flavour.
green the hottest of the traditional pastes; particularly good in chicken and vegetable curries, and a great addition to stir-fries and noodle dishes.

EGGPLANT also called aubergine. Ranging in size from tiny to very large and in colour from pale green to deep purple. Can also be purchased char-grilled, packed in oil, in jars.

EGGS we use large chicken eggs weighing an average of 60g unless stated otherwise in the recipes in this book. If a recipe calls for raw or barely cooked eggs, exercise caution if there is a salmonella problem in your area, particularly in food eaten by children and pregnant women.

FENNEL also called finocchio or anise; a crunchy green vegetable slightly resembling celery that's eaten raw in salads; fried as an accompaniment; or used as an ingredient in soups and sauces. Also the name given to the dried seeds of the plant which have a stronger licorice flavour.

FIVE-SPICE POWDER although the ingredients vary from country to country, five-spice is usually a fragrant mixture of ground cinnamon, cloves, star anise, sichuan pepper and fennel seeds. Used in Chinese and other Asian cooking; available from most supermarkets or Asian food shops.

FRENCH-STYLE GREEN LENTILS related to the famous french lentils du puy; these green-blue, tiny lentils have a nutty, earthy flavour and a hardy nature that allows them to be rapidly cooked without disintegrating. Are also known as australian, bondi or matilda lentils.

GNOCCHI Italian 'dumplings' made of potatoes, semolina or flour; can be boiled or baked with sauce.

GREEN ONION also known as scallion or (incorrectly) shallot; an immature onion picked before the bulb has formed, with a long, bright-green edible stalk.

HARISSA a North African paste made from dried red chillies, garlic, olive oil and caraway seeds; can be used as a rub for meat, an ingredient in sauces and dressings, or eaten as a condiment for tagines and grills.

KAFFIR LIME LEAVES also known as bai magrood and looks like two glossy dark green leaves joined end to end, forming a rounded hourglass shape. Sold fresh, dried or frozen, the dried leaves are less potent so double the number if using them as a substitute for fresh; a strip of fresh lime peel may be substituted for each kaffir lime leaf.

KUMARA the Polynesian name of an orange-fleshed sweet potato often confused with yam; good baked, boiled, mashed or fried similarly to other potatoes.

LEEKS a member of the onion family, the leek resembles a green onion but is much larger and more subtle in flavour. Tender baby or pencil leeks can be eaten whole with minimal cooking but adult leeks are usually trimmed of most of the green tops then chopped or sliced and cooked as an ingredient in stews and soups.

MAPLE SYRUP distilled from the sap of sugar maple trees found only in Canada and about 10 states in the USA. Maple-flavoured syrup or pancake syrup is not an adequate substitute for the real thing.

MILK we always use full-cream homogenised milk unless specified.
buttermilk in spite of its name, buttermilk is actually low in fat, varying between 0.6 per cent and 2.0 per cent per 100ml. Originally the term given to the slightly sour liquid left after butter was churned from cream, today it is intentionally made from no-fat or low-fat milk. Because it is low in fat, it's a good substitute for dairy products such as cream or sour cream in some baking and salad dressings.

NIGELLA SEEDS also called kalonji or black onion seeds. Tiny, angular seeds, black on the outside and creamy within, with a sharp nutty flavour that is enhanced by frying briefly in a dry hot pan before use. Sometimes erroneously called black cumin seeds.

PAPRIKA ground dried sweet red capsicum (bell pepper); many grades and types are available, including sweet, hot, mild and smoked.

PASTRY, PACKAGED
fillo is unique in that no fat or margarine is added to the dough. The dough is very elastic in texture and not rolled like other pastries but stretched to the desired thickness. Brush with butter or oil before baking.
puff pastry packaged sheets of frozen puff pastry, available from supermarkets.
shortcrust pastry packaged sheets of frozen shortcrust pastry, available from supermarkets.

PERSIAN FAIRY FLOSS usually labelled pashmak from the Persian for "little wool", this is a fairy floss (cotton candy) made from sesame and sugar.

PISTACHIOS green, delicately flavoured nuts inside hard off-white shells. Available salted or unsalted, in their shells or shelled.

POLENTA also known as cornmeal; a flour-like cereal made of dried corn (maize). Also the dish made from it.

PROSCIUTTO a kind of unsmoked Italian ham; salted, air-cured and aged, it is usually eaten uncooked. There are many styles of prosciutto, one of the best being Parma ham, from Italy's Emilia Romagna region, which is traditionally lightly salted, dried then eaten raw.

QUINCE yellow-skinned fruit with hard texture and astringent, tart taste; eaten cooked or as a preserve. Long, slow cooking makes the flesh a deep rose pink.

ROCKET also called arugula, rugula and rucola; peppery green leaf eaten raw in salads or used in cooking. Baby rocket leaves are smaller and less peppery in flavour.

ROSE PETALS freeze dried rose petals are edible and make great cake and dessert decorations.

SAFFRON stigma of a member of the crocus family, available ground or in strands; imparts a yellow-orange colour to food once infused. The quality can vary greatly; the best is the most expensive spice in the world.

SAUCES
fish called naam pla on the label if Thai-made, nuoc naam if Vietnamese; the two are almost identical. Made from pulverised salted fermented fish (most often anchovies); has a pungent smell and strong taste. Available in varying degrees of intensity, so use according to your taste.
plum a thick, sweet and sour dipping sauce made from plums, vinegar, sugar, chillies and spices.
soy also known as sieu; made from fermented soybeans. Several varieties are available in supermarkets and Asian food stores; we use Japanese soy sauce unless indicated otherwise.
worcestershire thin, dark-brown spicy sauce developed by the British when in India; used as a seasoning for meat, gravies and cocktails, and also as a condiment.

SEAFOOD
blue-eye also known as deep sea trevalla or trevally and blue-eye cod; thick, moist white-fleshed fish.
ling a member of the cod family with white, firm, moist flesh; fillets are nearly boneless.
prawns also known as shrimp. Varieties include, school, king, royal red, sydney harbour, tiger. Can be bought uncooked (green) or cooked, with or without shells.
smoked cod white fish with a milky smoky flavour; skin orange coloured.
white fish means non-oily fish; includes bream, flathead, whiting, snapper, dhufish, redfish and ling.

SESAME SEEDS black and white are the most common of this small oval seed, however there are also red and brown varieties. The seeds are used as an ingredient and as a condiment. Roast the seeds in a heavy-based frying pan over low heat.

SHALLOTS also called french shallots, golden shallots or eschalots. Small and elongated, with a brown-skin, they grow in tight clusters similar to garlic.

SILVER BEET also known as swiss chard and incorrectly, spinach; has fleshy stalks and large leaves, both of which can be prepared as for spinach.

SPECK smoked pork.

SPINACH also known as english spinach and incorrectly, silver beet. Baby spinach leaves are best eaten raw in salads; the larger leaves should be added last to soups, stews and stir-fries, and should be cooked until barely wilted.

SPRING ROLL WRAPPERS also known as egg roll wrappers; they come in various sizes and can be purchased fresh or frozen. Made from a delicate wheat-based pastry, they can be used for making gow gee and samosas as well as spring rolls.

SUGAR we use coarse, granulated table sugar, also known as crystal sugar, unless otherwise specified.
brown a soft, finely granulated sugar retaining molasses for its characteristic colour and flavour.
caster also known as superfine or finely granulated table sugar.
demerara small-grained golden-coloured crystal sugar.
icing also known as confectioners' sugar or powdered sugar; pulverised granulated sugar crushed together with a small amount of cornflour.
palm also called nam tan pip, jaggery, jawa or gula melaka; made from the sap of the sugar palm tree. Light brown to black in colour and usually sold in rock-hard cakes; use brown sugar if unavailable.

TAHINI sesame seed paste available from Middle Eastern food stores.

TOMATOES
bottled tomato pasta sauce a prepared tomato-based sauce (sometimes called ragu or sugo on the label); comes in varying degrees of thickness and kinds of spicing.
canned whole peeled tomatoes in natural juices.
egg also called plum or roma, these are smallish, oval-shaped tomatoes much used in Italian cooking or salads
paste triple-concentrated tomato puree used to flavour soups, stews, sauces and casseroles.
sauce also known as ketchup

WHITE BEANS a generic term we use for canned or dried cannellini, haricot, navy or great northern beans belonging to the same family, Phaseolus vulgaris.

WONTON WRAPPERS similar to gow gee or spring roll pastry sheets, made of flour, egg and water, are found in the refrigerated or freezer section of Asian food shops and many supermarkets.

YEAST (dried and fresh), a raising agent used in dough making. Granular (7g sachets) and fresh compressed (20g blocks) yeast can almost always be substituted one for the other when yeast is called for.

YOGURT we use plain full-cream in our recipes unless specifically noted otherwise. If a recipe in this book calls for low-fat yogurt, we use one with a fat content of less than 0.2 per cent.

ZUCCHINI also called courgette; small, pale- or dark-green or yellow vegetable of the squash family. Harvested when young, its edible flowers can be stuffed with a mild cheese and deep-fried.

conversion chart

MEASURES

One Australian metric measuring cup holds approximately 250ml; one Australian metric tablespoon holds 20ml; one Australian metric teaspoon holds 5ml.

The difference between one country's measuring cups and another's is within a two- or three-teaspoon variance, and will not affect your cooking results. North America, New Zealand and the United Kingdom use a 15ml tablespoon.

All cup and spoon measurements are level. The most accurate way of measuring dry ingredients is to weigh them. When measuring liquids, use a clear glass or plastic jug with the metric markings.

We use large eggs with an average weight of 60g.

DRY MEASURES

METRIC	IMPERIAL
15g	½oz
30g	1oz
60g	2oz
90g	3oz
125g	4oz (¼lb)
155g	5oz
185g	6oz
220g	7oz
250g	8oz (½lb)
280g	9oz
315g	10oz
345g	11oz
375g	12oz (¾lb)
410g	13oz
440g	14oz
470g	15oz
500g	16oz (1lb)
750g	24oz (1½lb)
1kg	32oz (2lb)

LIQUID MEASURES

METRIC	IMPERIAL
30ml	1 fluid oz
60ml	2 fluid oz
100ml	3 fluid oz
125ml	4 fluid oz
150ml	5 fluid oz
190ml	6 fluid oz
250ml	8 fluid oz
300ml	10 fluid oz
500ml	16 fluid oz
600ml	20 fluid oz
1000ml (1 litre)	1¾ pints

LENGTH MEASURES

METRIC	IMPERIAL
3mm	⅛in
6mm	¼in
1cm	½in
2cm	¾in
2.5cm	1in
5cm	2in
6cm	2½in
8cm	3in
10cm	4in
13cm	5in
15cm	6in
18cm	7in
20cm	8in
22cm	9in
25cm	10in
28cm	11in
30cm	12in (1ft)

OVEN TEMPERATURES

The oven temperatures in this book are for conventional ovens; if you have a fan-forced oven, decrease the temperature by 10-20 degrees.

	°C (CELSIUS)	°F (FAHRENHEIT)
Very slow	120	250
Slow	150	300
Moderately slow	160	325
Moderate	180	350
Moderately hot	200	400
Hot	220	425
Very hot	240	475

The imperial measurements used in these recipes are approximate only. Measurements for cake pans are approximate only. Using same-shaped cake pans of a similar size should not affect the outcome of your baking. We measure the inside top of the cake pan to determine sizes.

index

First published in 2011 by ACP Magazines Ltd,

a division of Nine Entertainment Co.

54 Park St, Sydney

GPO Box 4088, Sydney, NSW 2001.

phone (02) 9282 8618; fax (02) 9267 9438

acpbooks@acpmagazines.com.au; www.acpbooks.com.au

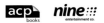

ACP BOOKS

General Manager - Christine Whiston

Associate Publisher - Seymour Cohen

Editor-in-Chief - Susan Tomnay

Creative Director - Hieu Chi Nguyen

Food Director - Pamela Clark

Published and Distributed in the United Kingdom by Octopus Publishing Group

Endeavour House

189 Shaftesbury Avenue

London WC2H 8JY

United Kingdom

phone (+44)(0)207 632 5400; fax (+44)(0)207 632 5405

info@octopus-publishing.co.uk;

www.octopusbooks.co.uk

Printed by Toppan Printing Co., China

International foreign language rights - Brian Cearnes, ACP Books bcearnes@acpmagazines.com.au

A catalogue record for this book is available from the British Library.

ISBN 978-1-74245-0704

© ACP Magazines Ltd 2011

ABN 18 053 273 546